P9-CMN-700

Letters from the Farm

Letters from the Farm

A Simple Path for a Deeper Spiritual Life

Peace & Love
Becca Stevens

BECCA STEVENS

Morehouse Publishing
NEW YORK

Copyright © 2015 by Becca Stevens

All rights reserved. No part of this book may be reproduced, stored in a retrieval system, or transmitted in any form or by any means, electronic or mechanical, including photocopying, recording, or otherwise, without the written permission of the publisher.

Unless otherwise noted, the Scripture quotations contained herein are from the New Revised Standard Version Bible, copyright © 1989 by the Division of Christian Education of the National Council of Churches of Christ in the U.S.A. Used by permission. All rights reserved.

Scriptures marked (KJV) are from the King James Version of the Bible.

Morehouse Publishing, 19 East 34th Street, New York, NY 10016
Morehouse Publishing is an imprint of Church Publishing Incorporated.

www.churchpublishing.org

Cover design by Laurie Klein Westhafer
Typeset by Beth Oberholtzer

Library of Congress Cataloging-in-Publication Data
Stevens, Becca, 1963-
    Letters from the farm : a simpler path for a deeper spiritual life / Becca Stevens.
        pages   cm
    ISBN 978-0-8192-3175-8 (pbk.) -- ISBN 978-0-8192-3176-5
(ebook) 1. Spiritual life. 2. Love. I. Title.
BV4832.3.S738   2015
248.4--dc23
2015002681

Printed in the United States of America

Dedication

On May 19, 2014, twenty-five people were baptized in the Harpeth River in the hills of Tennessee. The joy present in the cold waters washed over me and stands out as one of the finest days of my ministry. To witness such abundance and beauty in the river alongside a pristine farm on the sunniest day of the year was breathtaking—almost more than a heart can bear in real time. Each family came with their own sorrows and fears alongside their hopes, but down by the riverside those were laid aside for a minute. In those freezing cold and fast waters we simply felt the rich blessing of new life. For a moment we all held on to one another, trying to embrace an eternal love through our temporal bodies.

I want to remember that day forever without trivializing or tying it up in a neat package. I want to remember feeling caught in the current as the Spirit descended as we stood together holding on. I dedicate this book to the story of rebirth of twenty-five people in the hopes that the following letters help them on their journey ahead. James McClellan Barbieri, James Cummings Berry, Genevieve Adele Bieck, Charles Montgomery Buntin, Preston Oakes Cross, Landen Crouch, Julia Bolling Dryden, Leland Monaghan Eadie, Robert Cooper Feldman, John Duncan Feldman, Thomas Lawson Foster, Mei Ishii, Minami Ishii, Taiyou Ishii, Wendell Theron Karns, Madelyn Hayes McGowan, Jude Francis Nardella, Charles Waller Robbins, Wendy Ann Southard, Henry Boardman Stewart III, Daniel Tashian, Matilda Tashian, Tinkerbell Tashian, Tigerlily Tashian, and Edwin Bass Tyler.

I am not more faithful than when I was twenty.
I am filled with the same doubts and fears.
It's just that now I live
into my faith more than my doubts
and pray to walk with a heart wide open;
To live into the hope that love is eternal,
and allow the course of the river to carry me,
instead of trying to swim upstream.

—BECCA STEVENS

Contents

Winter

Acknowledgments

A special thank you to my colleagues who offered editorial advice and edits, including Perry Macdonald, Don Welch, and Susan Sluser. Thank you to Nancy Bryan from Church Publishing, who came to Nashville and helped me decide that I wanted to write this book. Tim, as always, without your commitment and love, there is no book. Sandy, Mary, Lissa, Connally and Kathi, without your leadership of the Boards we would be lost on the farm. Donna, Holli, Jim, Anna, Regina, Sheila, Courtney, Fiona, Abi, Gaile, Anika, Shana, Jennifer, Dorris, Marlei, Katrina, Chelle, Peggy, Deb, Peggy, Tara, Cathy, Andrew, Kay, Brenda, Scott, Michael, Nicholas, Gideon, Frannie, Francie, Chris, you drive the plow with grace. To all the volunteers and communities around the world supporting this work, keep watering and weeding: we need you. To Marcus, Levi, Caney, and Moses, I love you all dearly. The hope is that the following letters helps us all walk the path with intention and grace as we all make our way to the shore. Thank you to the staff of Magdalene, Thistle Farms, The Thistle Stop Café, Shared Trade, the Center for Contemplative Justice, St. Augustine's, and their boards. Thank you to all the people who offered such amazing hospitality to the community of Thistle Farms and my family on our global farm journey. Thank you to all the people who offered me forgiveness for the speed of my travel and the shortcomings of my gratitude. Thank you to the great bloggers who have helped us grow a movement for women's freedom and for all the people who have bought our products and shared our message that love is the most powerful force for change in the world. The world is truly our farm and the harvest is plentiful. Thank you, thank you, thank you.

Introduction

The following are letters from a farm that is as much a state of mind as a place. The letters are written for young priests, old friends, survivors who have been trafficked, and anyone seeking to live grounded in the belief that love heals. We can cut deep furrows and create rich beds for growing when we are not blinded by the bright lights of ego, sidetracked by the illusion of power, and stuck in the mud of inaction, feeling defeated or overwhelmed. We all have stepped in unseen holes, and found ourselves digging on hard, rocky ground. I have learned so much about farming both practically and spiritually from the work of Thistle Farms, a national bath and body care manufacturing and distribution enterprise run by survivors of trafficking and addiction that I founded in 2001. I have also gained a bit of wisdom from great leaders along the way who have been willing to share their hearts. I have seen that the people who work with integrity tend their fields in a posture of gratitude and I have tried to learn to farm that way too. It has been a gift to use tools left by other farmers that help me cultivate a sense of courage, inspiration, humility, forgiveness, compassion, and faithfulness. The hardest part about beginning this book was imagining the recipients of these letters. Am I writing to a class of seminarians preparing to embark on a vocation of service? Am I writing to a grieving father who is just about sick of religious platitudes and sweet sentiments? Am I writing to my own children who may at some point after my death want to know what I was thinking trying to establish sanctuaries and social enterprises for women who have survived prostitution, addiction, and trafficking? I hope that I am writing to someone who has not let the cynical part of their heart abandon the search for the place where justice and faith intersect. Maybe I am writing to a lonely seeker of community who knows that even though we make the journey alone, we can walk with each other. Perhaps there is a priest needing a story for a sermon. If I were betting on who picks up this book, I bet it's "square pegs," drummers who hear a beautiful rhythm all their own, and folks who have known some brokenness in their own lives. I am writing to myself too. It is such a gift to reflect on the lessons learned founding and running the place called Thistle Farms.

These letters from the farm describe a faith that strives for justice and peace through loving our neighbors. It began with the simple hope that love can help in community. That hope led to a social enterprise called Thistle Farms and that led to learning that we reap a hundredfold the seeds that are sown in a loving community. I became a student of herbs, teas, and trees because of my work with women. I am a farmer, not because I grow plants well, but because I love all of creation and tend to the parts of it in my own vineyard. Healing on this path is the central sacrament.

In the end, I always feel that I am just trying to write a love letter to God. That is what I imagine I am doing with this book—writing a love letter that is simple and compelling to folks seeking a deeper faith as they work in the fields and vineyards of their lives, creating a compassionate community and rich environment that encourages us to see the fruits of our labors.

Peace and love,

Becca

A note about format: Accompanying each letter is a verse of Scripture and some questions for reflection so that this book may be used as a devotional guide as well as a piece to inspire you in your faith and life. I have also included some prayers that might be helpful if there are groups reading these letters together.

Begin with Dirt
From a Geranium Field in Rwanda

Listen! A sower went out to sow. And as he sowed, some seeds fell on the path, and the birds came and ate them up. Other seeds fell on rocky ground, where they did not have much soil, and they sprang up quickly, since they had no depth of soil. But when the sun rose, they were scorched; and since they had no root, they withered away. Other seeds fell among thorns, and the thorns grew up and choked them. Other seeds fell on good soil and brought forth grain, some a hundredfold, some sixty, some thirty.

MATTHEW 13:3B–8

This letter is written to folks who walk through this world feeling a bit lost. It is both a prayer and a reminder that we can never be truly lost because we are always part of the farm no matter where we are. We have stardust coursing through our veins, oceans for tears, and dirt in our bones. "We are dirt and to dirt we shall return" is the mantra of faith. That is the humbling and freeing truth of the human condition. An old friend used to express it more gently by saying that all our journeys begin and end with God. The first of these letters begins with the simple remembrance that we are made from earth. The gift of our lives is to prepare our soil to bear good fruit and then let it all go. It is what holds the world together and makes us a family.

Over the years I have fallen in love with dirt. I have no idea when it began; maybe in my childhood. Maybe it was the morning glories that trumpeted in the summer mornings like a faithful muse. They would climb out of the ground from volunteer seeds scattered the spring before. Maybe it was watching the transplanted black-eyed Susans grow from a small bundle that didn't look like it could live to take over a garden. It could have been the first time I grew a carrot and imagined magic taking place beneath the dirt as my carrot was forming like a flower bouquet hidden beneath a magician's colored scarf.

I have thought of dirt daily since I began thinking about writing these letters from the farm. I have thought about the red clay dirt in the American south, the rich black soil found in the north, and the dusty earth of the deserts where I have walked. I especially think of dirt when I am in places like Botswana, Uganda, and Rwanda. When you drive in a car there it is necessary to alternate between rolling the windows up and rolling them back down because while it's hot in the car, it's worse to have the dirt that's kicked up from the road blowing into the car. Dirt is a constant topic of conversation: is it dry season or wet season?

When my family and I were in Rwanda this year, we drove for hours down bumpy dirt roads to geranium fields. The dusty red dirt layered our clothes and skin, reminding us that dirt has always been here. We drove to the fields where women survivors of the genocide have formed a cooperative to grow geranium. This cooperative has been a partner of Thistle Farms for more than six years and supplies us with geranium as well as eucalyptus, lemon grass, and patchouli. We saw the places in the fields where twenty years ago women on their knees dug up the bones of those they loved who had been murdered and buried in the fields. Now they are still kneeling in that same dirt, digging up weeds and rocks to plant a field of herbs that will become the healing oils Thistle Farms uses in all our products. The planting and tending of these crops for more than a decade has produced such rich soil that things grow thirty- and sixtyfold. We are visiting this year in the dry season and watch as some of the women spend all day on a foot pump, watering so that the geranium can thrive. The bright cloth of the workers' clothing, rich green herbs, and the distinctive smell of manure fill the senses. In this space it is all about dirt and there is only farming. Only growing, weeding, tending, and reaping. It feels so simple and beautiful sitting in the field.

It makes sense that Jesus was all about dirt. He wrote notes in the dirt in the face of danger, used dirt to make a healing mud, and told the disciples to shake it off their feet when they found no peace in a town. In the heart of Matthew's Gospel Jesus is in the thick of dirt. He is giving the disciples a road map of how to travel into cities, preaching and teaching. He is focused on dirt and seeds and what needs to be rooted and tilled and tended in the midst of foreign occupation, poverty, hostility. It is so radical. There is so much injustice, so many principalities to rail against and instead he preaches about dirt and seeds. You think he is going to condemn the institutions and maybe demand some kind of military revolution to fight against the oppression. Instead he focuses four parables in a row on something very different: the dirt and seeds growing in us. He starts with the idea of plucking seeds on the Sabbath, then talks about the sower and the seed, then about those who put the weeds among the wheat, and finally about the mustard seed.

I wonder if the disciples weren't puzzled about why he was so focused on dirt and seeds. The lesson of the sower may be one of the most radical in the Gospel. Jesus is turning the soil to uncover roots, to find out what is really planted in our souls. He is inviting us to grow good fruit and to weep at the parched nature of our being. We need to till the earth of our hearts, watering it and weeding the unruly places that cause us to stumble. Dirt is universal and timeless, thank God. Dirt is the community in which all things grow.

There is something about a field where forgiveness, hope, and memory are sown. There is something particularly beautiful about a field that has known death beginning to grow new life. The soil and seeds Jesus describes are the same soil and seeds that we are standing in, here in Rwanda. This farm reminds me that the dirt in the parable is connected to this dirt and all the soil is connected as well. One person does not get good seed and good soil and another just rocky ground or a path. It's all part of the same ground and only in community can that dirt become rich soil. There have to be seasons wherein you lie fallow. All soil is worthless unless we work together to cultivate it. If I try to farm alone, the soil I tend will be parched in a matter of months. The Good News is not so much that rich soil can produce a hundredfold, it is that the rocky, parched, and weedy soil of this world and in my heart can bear new life. Working together, remembering that we are all dirt, makes it possible for all of us to cultivate the good soil of a life of faith. All soil is connected. Rocky soil becomes aerated by digging up roots and rocks, and using compost to make it rich. Dry soil becomes fertile with water and thin soil, easily scorched, becomes thick by building up beds, digging ditches for irrigation, and allowing seasons to lie fallow. Dirt will be our companion our whole lives; together we can make a rich field that will bear unbelievably sweet fruit.

> God stir the soul. Run the ploughshare deep. Cut the furrows round and round, overturn the hard, dry ground, spare no strength nor toil, even though I weep. In the loose, fresh mangled earth, sow new seed. Free of withered vine and weed, bring fair flowers to birth. Amen. —*Prayer from Singapore Church Missionary Society.*

QUESTIONS FOR REFLECTION

1. How would you describe the "soil" from which you or your community has sprung?

2. How is God calling you to tend and cultivate this soil?

It's Not What You Believe, It's How You Live

*From the Healing Garden at
Thistle Farms, Nashville, Tennessee*

◟◞ All who believed were together and had all things in common; they would sell their possessions and goods and distribute the proceeds to all, as any had need. Day by day, as they spent much time together in the temple, they broke bread at home and ate their food with glad and generous hearts.

ACTS 2:44–46

This letter should simply be addressed: *Dear child of God*. When a drunk driver killed my father, when I was five, my mom immediately became the single, poor mother of five children at the age of thirty-five. Mom says one of her memories of those first weeks was the outpouring of letters from friends who had heard the news. Someone addressed a letter to her with the simple salutation: "Dear child of God." She said it was about all she remembered from the many notes of sympathy. It must have reminded her that she was not outside the realm of grace and protection as a child of God, that there was still a child in her that belonged to a loving family, and that the weight of the world was indeed not on her shoulders. So when I receive letters from people asking advice about starting a social enterprise or speaking their truth about their brokenness, sometimes I have the clarity to address my notes back to them: *Dear child of God*.

I got a note recently from a young man asking some of the basic and important questions of faith. The questions he asked felt both innocent and universal: Is there really a place called heaven? Do I have to believe in the virgin birth? What does it mean to say you believe in resurrection? Huge questions all contained in one fairly short Saturday morning e-mail.

It's one of the sweeter e-mails you get as a priest when somebody is willing to trust you with the basic questions of faith; it is a gift not to be taken lightly. I took a walk and thought about the best way to respond in love to this beautiful letter. As I walked, there was a surprise spring "snowstorm" created by a stand of cottonwood trees. The cotton was flying everywhere. There were places where the down was two inches thick, covering the trail like a cumulus cloud. It felt just like the surprise of resurrection, when all of creation pours out joy and wonder in the midst of our lives. We all walk around like this young man with his questions or the disciples after the resurrection, wondering what we are supposed to believe and what we are supposed to say about our beliefs. Every one of the Gospels contains the tender and beautiful truth: we cannot fathom resurrection.

In Mark 16, after the resurrection, Mary Magdalene and one of the disciples go back to tell the story and none of the other disciples believe. In John 20, all the disciples are gathered in a room together. None of them recognize the risen Lord among them. In Luke 24, the beloved disciples walk the road to Emmaus and cannot fathom the idea that love is not dead. They do not suspect that it is Jesus incarnate among them. Miles and miles they walk together. All four gospels share the story that the community closest to our Lord cannot fathom resurrection. Do you remember the story when Peter gets up and reminds the scattered flock of what the old prophets and Joel had said (Acts 2)? "Your young men and women will prophesy. Your young men will see visions and your old men will dream dreams. The Spirit of the Lord will be upon the men and the women to see and speak this truth." Then he goes on to talk about what David did. David rejoiced in his heart because the presence of God was with him. Peter goes on to say that the community needs to do three things—be in fellowship, live in generosity, and break bread. That should be the response, he says, to the unfathomable truth of resurrection. It is not "tell me what it is I have to believe." That has never been the journey of communities coming together. The most beautiful prayer in the whole Gospel is, "Lord, help my unbelief."

The fellowship Peter spoke of brings us together and we see resurrected love all around us, especially in places we did not expect. We see it in falling cottonwood. We see it on strangers' faces. We see it when we thought people were dead and they come to new life in the understanding that love heals. That is what fellowship and community do: we love each other with radical hospitality, without judgment, and we watch each other spring to new life. This young man's heart will not be changed by reciting the letter of the law; it will be opened through experiencing the spirit of the law.

The second aspect of the early communities following the resurrection was to live in the hope of generosity. That is how that community was marked. Everything we grow in the gardens at the Thistle Farms' residences and everything we offer as gifts to residents and graduates is the result of the generosity and love of a whole community. Every woman who graces the door gets a huge basket. Every year there are retreats, new clothes, matched savings, and gourmet meals . . . all because people give in gratitude for all the mercy they have known. The generosity of community grounded in love is unbelievable. When we experience the generosity of a community over many years, we don't need to know another thing about their beliefs, really. Those actions tell us what we need to know about each other: that we can live in fellowship with deep generosity and we will not have need if we can share with a generous spirit.

And finally, a community's faithfulness is known by the breaking of the bread. There is beauty in the breaking of the bread when we feel fed, not judged, accepted for who we are. My prayer for community is to keep breaking bread together, finding room for all of us around this altar so that we can go into the world surprised by all the ways resurrected love looks and acts.

So, while the letters from young seekers and questions from the depths of our own hearts will always arise, we remember it is not what we say, it is how we live. We are called to faithfulness by living generously with one another, in fellowship, around the breaking of the bread.

Shana, a leader of the sales team at Thistle Farms, was born into addiction, sold into prostitution about the age of twelve, and trafficked around the United States. At fifteen, she tattooed across her chest "Trust No One." She says that she didn't believe anyone could help her, that God loved her and that she knew better than to trust anything. Finally, after years of addiction, abuse, and heartbreak, she found her way to Thistle Farms. She came into the residential community and learned that the biggest lie that she'd ever been told (after dropping out of school in sixth grade) was that she was stupid. She can run spreadsheets and track 430 stores like nobody's business. She has helped grow the retail aspects of Thistle Farms by more than 70 percent over the last two years. Her first year here was the first time she had celebrated Christmas sober since she was a small girl. It was her first time to actually make a wish list of some things she would like. The first time to ask for anything and think there is a chance in hell you will get it.

While all of us were stressing about the demands of retail at Christmas, we still held our daily circle. The circle is a sacred space where we begin every workday at Thistle Farms. We light a candle and remember all the women still on the streets, still in prisons and jails, all looking for a way home. My hope that particular day was to hurry up and finish with the meditation circle so we could get on with the work. But then Shana stood up in the middle of circle and did the first cartwheel of her life. If you have never seen an adult woman do her first cartwheel, it is stunning. That cartwheel was the culmination of years of work and willingness to fumble in the dark, trusting that the path will appear. The spinning in the circle was like resurrection itself. Watching her, I understood that she knew she could trust that everyone in that circle loved her. Shana hadn't come into the community believing she would one day be free enough to do a cartwheel. It was the hard work she had done—living in fellowship, sharing what she had, and participating in the recovery traditions—that allowed her the gift of flight for a moment.

QUESTIONS FOR REFLECTION

1. Whose actions show you the resurrection?
2. How has the breaking of bread and fellowship deepened your faith?

Pray to Get Out of the Way
San Francisco, California

⌁ And Peter took [Jesus] aside and began to rebuke him, saying, "God forbid it, Lord! This must never happen to you." But he turned and said to Peter, "Get behind me, Satan! You are a stumbling block to me; for you are setting your mind not on divine things but on human things."

MATTHEW 16:22-24

It would be a great gift to think of this letter having a butterfly effect of a peaceful presence somewhere in this world full of turmoil. The butterfly effect is the idea introduced in chaos theory that a small change can create a big difference. In other words, a butterfly can flap its wings in one part of the world, and the wind can be changed and may even cause a hurricane on the other side of the globe. The wishful hope is that a prayer for peace could change the balance of peace in this world. That a small act of love can change the balance of love. That our work could make a difference in this world. I understand why people get fearful in their role as a pastor or mentor: it can feel fraudulent, acting our parts as insightful gurus into the spiritual issues plaguing our world even as we are filled with hidden doubts in the face of injustice and oppression. Gratefully, there are times in the face of injustice and oppression when we move beyond ourselves and feel compelled to speak and act.

I am writing this letter and wishing for wisdom from a plane thirty-five thousand feet in the air. As we cut through clouds that look like tic-tac-toe patterns, I am trying to remember how I got here. I don't even like to fly, yet it seems that I am flying almost weekly now. I keep flying like I am going to get somewhere or become somebody, but wherever I land humility is often the lesson for the day—again. It is true that whenever we compare ourselves to anyone else, we find a false sense of confidence or are reminded of our shortcomings. But on this journey there is a break as we fly through the clouds and for just a minute I can float above the clumsy way I try to be funny or my awkwardness with introductions.

The journey through the clouds is like looking at our egos. It looks substantial enough to walk across until you find that the plane sails through with just a bit of turbulence. I am convinced that our egos carry about the same weight as a cloud. After years of visiting churches, I have learned that any feeling I carry into the community will be what I reap when my visit is over. If I carry bitterness or bruised ego, I will come out feeling a bit depressed and overwhelmed by the reception. If I carry in gratitude, I will meet new friends and open doors for the women coming with me from Thistle Farms. The honest-to-God truth is that I am liable to carry either one. If I get there and the pastor has decided he will preach and we will have the Sunday school hour to make our presentation, I can get my feelings hurt. If I arrive to discover big posters all around and folks are asking for books to be signed, I can get to feeling pretty good about myself. The truth is much simpler and both responses ring hollow in the midst of something deeper: it was never about me and it doesn't matter whether I am humbled or exalted. It was always supposed to be about love and helping the next woman find her way home. On the farm it is never about the farmer, it is always about the crop. We need to cultivate a farmer's ego.

So how is it that we can get out of the way enough as farmers to raise a decent crop? The first step may lie in the truth that there are only certain seasons for growing. If we have doubts about how well we are planting in the spring, we need to remember that when our crop is suffering in the summer and we have a scarce harvest. The second step is to get help with the planning and sowing of the seeds and that will help us remember that the harvest is not ours alone. The definition of wisdom surely contains the realization that we need to discern with others when we are not clear about the pathway forward. The third step is then to cultivate a grateful and pastoral heart for those who are walking alongside you on the farm.

The way to cultivate a beautiful crop with a community after we remove our ego and sow seeds of gratitude is to listen. If we can listen, our growth and the growth of a community will multiply exponentially. If I can hear you, then it means that the voices in my own head have quieted enough to get out the way to allow you to flourish. I need to pray daily, "God teach me to listen . . . to the person walking beside me, to the lessons in nature, to the voice of the stranger, and to the one I have considered my enemy."

Listening is the way we stop tripping over ourselves in the midst of trying to serve another. That means even when the person in front of us drones on or hurts our feelings, we simply listen and then respond with the word of love. It is a deep and simple spiritual practice. I wish more pastors, including myself, practiced it all the time. May this reminder take flight like a plane through the clouds and find a place on the shoulder of any of us suffering from ego to say simply, "It's about the other person, not you."

That is the gift of freedom in ministry. It frees us up to step into a hospital room without planning what we are going to say, but simply to listen and to be present. It offers us the gift of getting out of the way so the person we are serving can feel the Spirit moving into their words and life. Pray to get out of the way, and then practice what you pray.

QUESTIONS FOR REFLECTION

1. Who in your life is asking you to listen to them?

2. What stands in the way of that conversation?

Search for Purple in Nature as We Grope for God

Sewanee, Tennessee

◯＼ And why do you worry about clothing? Consider the lilies of the field, how they grow; they neither toil nor spin, yet I tell you, even Solomon in all his glory was not clothed like one of these.

MATTHEW 6:28-29

◯＼ So that they would search for God and perhaps grope for him and find him—though indeed he is not far from each one of us.

ACTS 17:27

A small group of students and nuns on the Cumberland Plateau have been growing lavender for distillation at Thistle Farms. They call their lavender growing "the living prayer project": their goal is to turn the mountain purple with lavender. The Sisters of St. Mary's, tucked away in Sewanee, Tennessee, have always been about bringing justice for women and sanctuary for those who have been abused. The students attend the University of the South, where a commitment to justice has a long, if uneven, history.

I have always searched for purple in nature. Purple is that royal and penitential hue that feels like it is the color of tenderness. Sometimes, in a field of wildflowers when I see purple and yellow flowers blooming together, it makes my jaw clench it is so lovely. I look for purple in the landscape just as others search for four-leaf clovers. It feels reassuring to see a lovely flower and remember the gospel call to the disciples to consider the wildflowers as a glimpse of the kingdom of God. In the midst of a world that is endlessly in turmoil and groping for God, it is a gift to see a purple flower and feel the indwelling of the Spirit.

The early apostles encountered a hostile world. The story of Christianity begins with a mission in which all the major players were imprisoned and Stephen had been martyred. It was a dramatic time for new apostles who had been chained for telling their truth. When Peter speaks to the community of Athens, he is amazed by their desire for dialogue and their faithfulness to what it is they see as truth. He stands before them and says, "You will search and indeed some of you will grope to find God only to discover God was never far from you." We grope and search and suddenly find that God was not far from us.

Dorothy Day, the founder of the Catholic Worker movement, who lived her life in search of what it means to give everything for the sake of love, entitled her autobiography *The Long Loneliness*. It was a search, a groping, to discover every now and then that God was right there. The Rev. Dr. Howard Thurman, who grew up in the South during the Jim Crow period, found himself not only drawn to social justice but to a powerful mysticism that says there is nothing better than to find this transcendent place of peace. The Rev. Dr. Martin Luther King Jr. describes in his writings the great revelation of his life, pondering over a single cup of coffee at midnight. For all three, the journey of a truth-seeker was one of loneliness reaching out beyond all boundaries, groping for truth. To find that space where God is right there, to discover again that God was never far from us. It is in the searching that we discover how close the Spirit really is. The search for purple and small signs of hope helps us to notice the great truth that God was never far from us.

There is one particular graduate of the Magdalene program who has traveled with me and describes with stunning accuracy how the groping for God can move one from the brink of hell to hope. She tells about the four months she spent locked in a closet by her abuser. She was let out to be raped by strangers and to use the restroom, but she lived in the closet with no bed, a blanket, and food and water. There was no light in the closet and she spent those four long months groping for everything. She describes a sliver of light visible at the bottom of the closet door that gave her just enough illumination to keep up hope in the world outside. She believes in the groping between the haze of drugs and the waves of fear that she could feel God right there beside her. As I hear her story of groping and feeling God's presence in the midst of such horror, I am filled with the assurance that God is close.

I felt that closeness to the Spirit of God not too long ago in the middle of the Harpeth River in middle Tennessee. It was so stunning that I dedicated this entire book to the experience. Twenty-five people went to the river to be baptized. While we were gathering in the water, we made a vow not to complain about the near-freezing temperature as the current rushed by. Then something happened I had never seen before. People were coming down with their babies and the whole family was going under the water together. It became a group activity. It was unbelievable. I don't know how to explain it. People were immersing themselves in the whole experience and as they came up out of the water, there would be this "wooshhh." I knew I was witnessing something I had never seen in twenty-three years of ordination and would probably never see again. The baptisms took place during Ascension week when the church celebrates Jesus's ascending to heaven. As we were in that river, I realized that the reason you can believe and proclaim ascension is not that somebody rises to heaven. It's that heaven reaches down and is not that far from us. Indeed, it is so close we can see it. You and I have been given this great gift.

Sometimes the gift of faith is that we get to feel that the Spirit is not so far from us. So, let the prayer be that you and

I see the holy in each other, that you see it in the people all around you, that you feel it walking around this beautiful gift we call creation. May we see it as the purple asters and irises blossom and as the sunset changes pink into a sweet lavender that whispers peace. May we feel the Spirit move the amazing gift we call our children. May our groping lead us into the profound sense of the eternal in our communion with one another. May our groping for the Spirit and our search for the royal and penitential purple shades of nature lead us to touch and recognize heaven in our lives.

I wonder sometimes if, by some miracle, as we cross over to the eternal side of time we will finally come to realize, "My God, it was never that far from us all along."

QUESTIONS FOR REFLECTION

1. Where in the landscape of your life do you see an expression of God's grace?

2. What is the "royal and penitential" color that speaks most to you?

Let Your Knees Buckle
with Gratitude
Pensacola, Florida

⌇⌇ O children of Zion, be glad and rejoice in the Lord your God; for he has given the early rain for your vindication, he has poured down for you abundant rain, the early and the later rain, as before. The threshing floors shall be full of grain, the vats shall overflow with wine and oil.

JOEL 2:23–24

It's wonderful to think that this letter might find its way to someone in prison. Sometimes we can't imagine joy from the slim window allowing us to see just a sliver of the vast landscape before us. Sometimes it is impossible to think that from a cell where we feel we are being punished, we are truly being freed. There was a woman who graced our threshold at Thistle Farms back in the 1990s who spent eight years during her twenties in prison. Four of those years were in solitary confinement in an eight-by-four-foot cell, twenty-three hours a day. When I asked her how she survived, she just laughed and said, "My God, I was in prison long before they ever locked the door." She went on to tell me about sleeping sitting in the bathtub to avoid being raped before sunrise and of the murders of her friends that left her so paralyzed with fear she would stay stoned for days on end.

Maybe the truth is that the deeper our fear cuts into our soul, the more gratitude it can contain. I do think that fear can transform into gratitude. I have seen it so many times that I am actually starting to believe it. I have seen women who were afraid that something was going to be taken away, or someone was going to get more, or that somehow they were going to mess up and be back on the streets; when finally those fears get laid to rest, they start to sing in gratitude for being released.

I remember one woman, six months clean, getting ready to tell her story for the first time. Her sexual abuse started young and she can't remember the names of all those who raped her before she was fifteen. It's hard to imagine so many abusers that you lose track of their names. It makes most of our abuse look tame. After she came to Thistle Farms, you could see that she was slowly healing the fear, turning it to gratitude like melting ice off an eave. She wrote the speech she wanted to give to a community thinking of opening a house for women with histories of trafficking. Before her speech, she was so nervous she wouldn't eat. Before she spoke, I told the crowd gathered that it was her first speech ever and it would be much easier to get the standing ovation out of the way at the beginning. She took the stage as everyone stood and applauded. As the spirit of fear left her and the whole community, everyone wept. Everyone. The weeping was like watching all our knees buckle together in gratitude that we are free of fear and can simply love one another. Watching her take in the applause was a witness to love and what God looks like standing before you. You could feel scales fall from eyes and tears of gratitude pour as minutes of rolling applause washed away everything but gratitude. On that day I could easily remember all the mercy people have shown us. Life is a gift, but our mortality can be balanced and strengthened by gratitude. Gratitude can carry us through dry seasons. Gratitude can allow us to feel rains fall on the parched landscape of our past. Gratitude can allow us to see the rich grains scattered on the threshing floors of our lives that we have overlooked. It is one of the great keys to peace and understanding. Be grateful, not because it is fair, but because you are beloved.

1. What are the fears that keep you from seeing the possibility of freedom?

2. What are the gifts of love and mercy for which you can be grateful?

Notice the Light
at the Eucharist
Wind River Reservation, Wyoming

〜 No one after lighting a lamp puts it under the bushel basket, but on the lampstand, and it gives light to all in the house.

MATTHEW 5:15

If you are a person who attends church or presides at an altar regularly, this letter is for you. It is to celebrate the routine of liturgy and the notion of common prayers that offer the spark that lights the lamp that we set on a lampstand. In almost every mosque, temple, and church, we put a light on a lampstand. Almost all of those sanctuaries have electricity, but we choose candlelight instead. We want to see the glow and watch the flame. We want to connect to the holy flicker of light and the way people have always worshiped. At Thistle Farms we have spent more than fifteen years making almost fifty thousand candles. We begin each morning lighting one of those candles, trusting that a single candle can light a path. In the right location, it is enough to bring another woman off the streets or out of prison. So we light a candle every day and put it on a lampstand for the whole community to see.

Whenever a candle is lit and placed in a meditation circle or on an altar, the first thing to do is notice the light. See how the flame dances or is still. Celebrate the haloed circles around the flame and notice how it plays off other light coming into the worship space. Every day it is different. As the familiar words and rituals begin, notice the unique light of this moment and set yourself firmly in the present.

One morning before the sun rose in a vast western sky where sunrises tend to take their time, I took a walk. I was waiting for the light as the gray sky left me yearning to see the pale rainbow of sunrise found in painted mountains. Time, normally rushing to grow children and deepen lines of worry, paused. There was no question which direction to walk; it's an instinct to turn toward the east where love rises in lilac over gray canvas. Once I could feel the light, I knew that I could be present for the women I would meet later that morning to talk about the possibility of starting a new social enterprise.

When I got to the meeting hall in the place called "the circle," the light poured into the room. The pale light of the morning was now burning bright yellow and warmed the whole room with broad beams that felt strong. There was already a great group of women from the reservation working together around the issues of violence and economic independence. It seemed there might be interest in partnering with Thistle Farms to generate new income for greater independence and healing. I was grateful the light was strong. There is so much beautiful work that women are currently doing for the Wind River community on health, stopping sexual violence, and recovery—social enterprise seemed the next logical step.

I brought with me sage, lavender, and other essential oils so we could make healing oils together as we got to know one another. As I sat down, I noticed that a beam of light had settled on the table in front of one of the women. On a blank piece of paper she had drawn a simple circle. There is probably not a better symbol to sum up the hope for women's social enterprise and sustaining community. "I was thinking," she said, pointing to the circle she had drawn, "that the old circle outside in the field isn't used much anymore. We could grow new things there."

It was a beautiful epiphany. We were on the place called "the circle," we were next to the church whose circular altar has not two, but just one candle in the center, and we were forming a circle slowly as women arrived. One of the recovery healers then began our time together by saying, "In the circle, women's tears are healing." I could feel a deep connection between this old and sacred circle and the circle we hold each morning at Thistle Farms, with our single candle and remembrance of women still on the streets. People yearn for a circle with a central light and I am grateful I got to be present in this one as it re-formed around this old tradition.

Soon we were talking through practical, organizational logistics. From there, ideas for product creation, attracting tourism, and welcoming children built on each other. One day, in our circle in Nashville, I will pull out a beaded vial of sage oil and set it next to the candle and remember all the prayers offered in that light.

When the orange globe peeks above the horizon in bursts of resurrection each morning, the moon takes a sweet bow. That light is the light of millions of candles and connects us all. We can walk with the sunrise preaching, "Walk with hope in faith because love lives." It's not that we are more faithful than we are in the dark of night; it's just that our pace is lighter. This translucent moment of clarity and hope is possible each day we do our work under that rising yellow force, or walk down a path at dawn humming a love song whose words are rising from our hearts, or remembering the courage of women on reservations preaching new hope. When we walk with this pace, we have the shadow of the sun before us like a benediction with an aftertaste of joy that is true gratitude for every day we have been given. On such mornings when our souls are turning into the color of time and we are reminded that one morning will be our last, we can feel the gift sink deep into our hearts.

When we follow the light, we can dance a jig that on this endless spinning earth, we have seen the light. Sunrise calls women with grieving hearts to sing; it enables priests to be present for decades at the same altar, and paints each morning in colors so tender they turn stone hearts to flesh. Light means that we can live in hope, dedicated to justice and truth, knowing the light will never leave us. The light is ours for the beholding and allows us to make our song even at our own Easter morning, "Alleluia, Alleluia, Alleluia."

QUESTIONS FOR REFLECTION

1. What are the times and places where light holds a special meaning for you?

2. Remembering a particularly dark time in your life, from where did the light come?

Let the Mission Form the Worship

From the Thistle Stop Café,
Nashville, Tennessee

God is spirit and those who worship him must worship in spirit and truth.

JOHN 4:24

This letter is borne out of a hope that the structures of the institutional church will continue to be challenged by creative and compassionate leaders. Nothing is set in stone: not liturgy, not words, and not communities. Too many times I have visited churches who have determined that their liturgy or structure will never change. The environment is lifeless: a beautiful still life, amazing to look at, hard to engage for a long time. This hope of creative leadership doesn't mean we don't embrace old liturgies and practices; it means we participate fully with our hearts and minds to give them—and us—new life. We let our daily work and practices help form how we worship just as our worship shapes our daily work. This challenge is going to have to be led by good ol' practical farmers who desire to grow a rich field of love in the world more deeply than they desire to preserve the form of the church. May it serve as a reminder to all of us that if we are not bearing good fruit in our lives of faith, we are not being truthful in our worship. Worship that is true and led by the Spirit calls us to confront with compassion the needs of the world and the community in which we serve. This means that our work in the world will bring new vision, life, resources into the church.

I didn't know when we started turning the soil to plant the seeds of Thistle Farms that this "farming" would also transform the way I see church and liturgy. Witness as we are to the injustice that comes from clinging to a dry bosom of Abraham, we should all want to shake it up a bit and rattle the cages that hold us back. Knowing the chasm that exists between what organized religion does and what it is capable of doing should call us all to work harder for justice. One of the many gifts the Thistle Farms community has given me is observing that the more leaders of congregations participate in efforts for justice, the more their communities are committed to one another and the united body of Christ. Now I see that the work of justice is the richest endeavor in the worship life of the community. Doing that work in the world every single week, whether I feel inspired or not, is the most inspired part of my own worship. It gives me a lens from which to enter the gospel; it keeps me praying to walk with courage and humility.

The community called St. Augustine's where I serve is now worth only 20 percent (in real dollars) of the current financial value of Thistle Farms. (St Augustine's Chapel serves the Vanderbilt community.) I believe that is a sign that we are heading down the right path. Working in the world and allowing our worship to be informed by that work means we are not afraid to engage the marketplace; we are able to reset financial priorities when they no longer prosper the mission; and we see love as a lavish business ideal, capable of transforming a community. We are called to be wanderers, continually seeking. Don't let the church "settle." Keep engaging and being willing to change.

QUESTIONS FOR REFLECTION

1. How does your work in the world, whatever it may be, inform how you worship?

2. How does your worship inform your work in the world?

The Light of Hope
Cuenca, Ecuador

〰 While it was still dark, Mary Magdalene came to the tomb and saw that the stone had been removed from the tomb.
JOHN 20:1

I hope that this letter can serve me as a reminder that hope rises as an unexpected joyful gift. I do not believe we can expect hope. I do not think we can create it. I do not believe we can extinguish hope. Hope lives in us and is a gift of grace that washes over us. It is by its nature a transformative reality of living into our greatest desires. If love heals and hope transforms, then it's helpful to remember that every dawn can break forth with a sense of hope. The first inklings of that sense of hope begin by remembering that sunrise starts before even the dawn. It was a slight change in tone that called Mary Magdalene to head to the garden. The story of the resurrection begins with the words, "While it was still dark." The light had not yet risen on the Sabbath as Mary headed out with grief as her guide to carry her to Jesus's body. Light, transformed from gray to pink like water to wine, is enough for her to see the stone rolled away and to run to Peter and John. As they run back to the tomb in a race with the murky light of dawn, they see enough to know Jesus is gone. Mary stands alone as the light breaks through and she sees angels and linen on the floor. Even though she cannot make out what she is seeing, she hears Jesus calling her. Then the light of hope fills her from within, and she reaches for Jesus.

It's hard to hope for resurrection, especially after crossing through wildernesses, bruised by thorns that caught us on the way. The wake of death casts a huge pall over dawns, and on those mornings, daybreak is a surprise, no matter how long we have waited and hoped. I can imagine Mary's surprise as the dawn poured light into the tomb and hope caught her unexpectedly. We all carry grief to the tombs of those we love. When I am most hopeful I find myself sitting in the chapel, sometimes before daylight. Keeping me company are the ashes of the departed faithful that rest inside the altar. On those mornings, as the light seeps into the chapel in unadulterated beams of white, I have felt hope rise with the sun. Sunrise in the story of Easter is not just a time of day; it is a state of the heart. Sunrise is the space where nighttime fears move aside for hope, where we feel peace about our mortality in the scope of the universal truth that love abides and where we feel light crest the dark horizons of hearts we have kept barricaded.

In the mountains of Ecuador, there is an eight-hundred-year-old marbled cathedral with stained-glass windows through which beams of light filter in the early morning. A visiting group from St. Augustine's visited this cathedral at the altar dedicated to Magdalene, there were indigenous women chanting prayers that carried this sunrise story of deep grief and unbounded hope through the rose-colored air. Several of us hovered near to catch a ray of that love story as we lit candles, wept for our friends and family who had died over the last year and felt hope rising in the truth that for thousands of years grieving hearts can sing.

Last week, as the sun was rising, I received an e-mail from a pastor whose ministry is caring for those who are HIV positive. He wrote about speaking with donors from the World Bank, asking them for continued financial support despite the fact that other funding is being pulled and the program is losing staff. It is so hard for him, but his courage and prophetic voice as a witness to justice and freedom for all people leads like a bright light. I wondered as I read the e-mail how he wrote with such hope in the midst of unfathomable obstacles. There was not an undertone of fear or aftertaste of fatigue. It was a hard e-mail about hope. He knows that people want to hope. We want to be called to see the light even in the dark times. The sun rises all over the world, all day long. And when we get a glimpse of its brightness, it is so beautiful it makes me weep.

When we follow in the footsteps of Magdalene, or even follow the example of the prophets today who preach hope in adverse times, we can dance a jig, signifying that on this endless spinning earth, we have seen the light.

QUESTIONS FOR REFLECTION

1. When in your life has light penetrated the darkness?
2. Where might you go today to share the news of this light?

Keep It Simple
St. Augustine's Chapel, Nashville, Tennessee

At that time Jesus said, "I thank you, Father, Lord of heaven and earth, because you have hidden these things from the wise and the intelligent and have revealed them to infants.

MATTHEW 11:25

This letter is written with kind thoughts holding up a young seeker, priest, parent, or writer who is earnest in her desire to share a good word. There is something holy about the people in this world who are still wild, searching, and open. My prayer is that the need to be found, tamed, or closed down never takes hold on those souls. Such seekers can keep a simpler faith, because not all of it needs to be explained as they can appreciate mystery in their search for meaning. When one doesn't need everything explained, what is preached and written about truth stays simpler. Keeping what we preach as simple as possible allows people to make their own conclusions and remember a bit of what you were trying to say. On any given Sunday, most people don't remember the vast majority of what you preached past their walk to the parking lot. The majority of those who do remember a bit of what was spoken while still in the parking lot forget most of the rest of what you said by the end of lunch. A good rule of thumb is that if you can't remember what you preach, no one else can either. This is not a depressing thought, it's actually very freeing. There is no need to waste hours fretting over what was said or left unsaid. Just try to preach your truth in love. Period.

People will remember simple things such as: if you preached with love emanating from your heart, if you were consistent in your message, and if you were wise enough to remember there is no "we" in opposition to "they" in preaching. So may this letter from a farm from servants and seekers serve as a reminder that you are free to speak your truth, clearly and simply, even if your voice shakes. It's been said that preachers basically have only one sermon; they just preach a thousand different versions of it. All of us do better the more we keep it simple and speak in stories.

I wish I knew how to keep it all really simple. Beyond just preaching, it is a great spiritual practice for all of us to keep it simple in our work. Doing the work of Thistle Farms amidst budget shortcomings, calendars, and personalities can feel very complicated. Remembering to keep the mission and message simple seems especially important since more than two-thirds of the employees suffer from post-traumatic stress disorder. Keeping it simple is akin to keeping it more peaceful. One of the easiest ways for us to keep it simple is to remember three G's for a deeper and more solid faith: Grieve fully, feel Gratitude profoundly, and be humble enough to do the Grunt work! That is it, really. It is that simple and that hard. We need to stay open enough to feel the grief of those who have died or left, we need to never forget the gratitude for all the mercy we have been given, and we need to always just do the grunt work and not complain about it!

Sometimes when we try to explain it more, we just dilute the message. And the message is simply Love heals.

QUESTIONS FOR REFLECTION

1. Which is the hardest of the three G's for you to practice to keep your faith simple? Grief, gratitude, or grunt work?

2. How can you attend to that difficulty in a way that helps you to embrace it?

Beggars in the Field

From a Speech to the House of Bishops in Nashville, Tennessee

⌇ She said, "Yes, Lord, yet even the dogs eat the crumbs that fall from their masters' table."

MATTHEW 15:27

I have often thought it felt like a strange scene stuck in the middle of the story, that as Jesus is talking with his disciples, a Canaanite woman boldly appears, begging for help. She famously banters with Jesus, reminding him, "even the dogs deserve the crumbs under the table." It's surprising that this one woman, just after he has fed more than five thousand people, is causing such a fuss. There they are, in the middle of a mission of healing, out in the middle of the field, and somehow this one woman begging for help is too much for the disciples; they ask Jesus to send her away.

This letter is to remind us all that we are beggars. The story of a Canaanite woman breaking rank and tradition by begging in the middle of Matthew's Gospel is a reminder that begging is in the middle of our faith. In the heart of Matthew's mission a beggar comes with hands out, needing help for her daughter. I swear it feels like the begging never ends. Jesus was right, "The poor will always be with you." The woman had no business or right asking for help, all she had was need. The Canaanite woman was so overwhelmed that her needs outweighed the disciples and their annoyance, so she forced her way toward Jesus to make her case. It is in the amazing exchange between healer and beggar that we learn that the place of charity in the life of faith is transformational. In the exchange between Jesus and the woman, the community huddled listening nearby realizes she is the proclaimer of the gospel. She was the preacher who offered crumbs of hope to a community in need of inspiration. She was the faithful one, one who reminds us still that a church without beggars is a museum. Indeed, we are beggars at an altar, grateful for the abundance of a crumb.

Beggars have been central to the ministry of the church and the reason for its existence. Thistle Farms' mission is centered on the belief that women who have survived the streets and prisons, who have wrestled addictions and withstood violence, proclaim mercy so profoundly that a whole community can find healing. There are many people reading this letter whose vocations are to recognize the profundity of begging for both the giver and receiver and how love is offered in the exchange. The faithful farmer must wrestle nobly with how to serve the beggar with integrity, how to love the Canaanite with dignity, and how to preach love without judgment.

Roy, who makes his way begging, has been a part of the chapel where I serve for twenty years. He has always depended upon folks for his survival. He and I are still debating if he lost his dentures or if someone stole them two weeks ago. Whatever happened, the loss of those teeth is a reminder that begging is a full-time job. Between transportation and finding caregivers, it takes a long time to replace lost items. Roy is doing it with his usual seesaw that leans first toward keen insight and wit and then back toward an internal mental struggle that I can't fathom. He tells me that twenty years ago he brought me to my work, that he built the church and blesses the work. That may be true. He always comes to church early, first to shower off the Saturday night street and then to fold the Sunday worship bulletins. Over the years I have seen him beg on Sunday mornings and have seen him handcuffed in the parking lot after cursing an officer. I have seen him with the staff, stretching their patience and watching them help. I have seen him be a faithful servant and then be so angry that I want to crawl under the altar and hide. After the chapel paid a portion of the cost of his teeth, I drove him to the synagogue up the street to get the next installment. I pulled off the road and after he got out of my car, he walked into the street and stopped traffic so I could back up without waiting. He is something. He cannot be contained by a program, diagnosis, or theology that asks us to simply serve the poor. He is the question in ministry, the embodiment of failed systems, the result of institutionalized poverty, and often the teacher. I love his walk, his sense of humor, and the fact that even when he gets banned or lost, he always comes home. He reminds me that "the poor will always be with you" is a blessing, not a curse.

Begging is not an issue to be solved, but a way we wrestle our way through injustices, oppression, poverty, and sickness. A faith without begging is an act. Begging is the fount of innumerable blessings. None of us are above or beneath begging. I have been begging my whole ministry. The crumbs under the table can fill our cups to overflowing with streams of gratitude and hope for this world. There are another hundred Canaanite women at the door. We will do well to remember we will probably be begging our whole lives for the sake of love.

QUESTIONS FOR REFLECTION

1. When have you begged? How did it feel?
2. Who are the beggars in your life? Do they make you uncomfortable?

The Holy Ground
of Farming
Inside St. Augustine's Chapel,
Barefoot

⌇⁓ Then he said, "Come no closer! Remove the sandals from your feet, for the place on which you are standing is holy ground."
EXODUS 3:5

It may be a simple symbolic gesture, but for me taking off my shoes helps to ground and settle me before I read Scripture, pray, or preach. I am writing this letter hoping that a few more folks will be willing to kick off their shoes and remember that all the ground on which we stand, farm, and worship is holy. When I take off my shoes, I remember all the bare feet exposed in the traditions of many faiths. The act helps me remember people have been taking off their shoes for thousands of years not just to keep the floor clean, but because it is a holy act. Being barefoot is a lesson in humility. To worship barefoot is understood only through practice. I have learned the lessons of going barefoot only by going barefoot, not by reading about it, talking about it, or thinking about it. When people ask, "Why don't you wear shoes?" my answer always feels a bit trite or self-serving. Still, after having spent years not wearing shoes, it makes more sense to me to ask, "Why do you keep your shoes on in church?" You learn so much more from taking them off than by just asking the question. Maybe asking the question though is the first step in slipping off the heels and tassels.

Recognizing that the ground is holy and "deshoeing" is a great first step toward helping us remember. Through taking off our shoes and feeling the cold linoleum or rugged stone, we remember our ancestors and that we are part of the ground upon which we walk. The ground gives life and is the source of much of what nourishes us our whole lives. When Moses stepped onto the holy ground, he felt God's presence in the bushes and offered his life in service in response. In the moment God asks Moses to remove his shoes, God is offering a way to be close to the earth and feel its holy fragility. That same offering is made to us. Feel the coldness, or the dust, or the small hidden stones. Walk more carefully and watch out for living creatures. Feel the balance and vulnerability of standing to walk paths that others have trod. They were surely barefoot in the vision of Eden from which all life sprang.

In South Africa they are said to have found "Eve's footprints," as the site is called. The footprints are more than a hundred thousand years old and of course, the person is barefoot. I imagine her as I sit barefoot to write this letter, walking toward water or gathering food. I imagine she knew somewhere deep in her bones that she was rooted to the earth she walked upon and that the soil was holy. In fact, she walked on such holy ground that her imprint is still seen. When you go to visit, there is very little pomp, just a sign near the indented flat rock that marked her passage. If we walked more like her, with her steady gate and knowing purpose, we might feel more at peace and less anxious. We might sink our feet into the sand and feel the wonder that those grains of sand eventually form sandstone, capable of holding our imprint. We might walk more carefully and with a greater respect for the land. We might have the courage to strip away the illusions that how we clothe ourselves and what we buy are somehow essential to who we are, setting us apart from one another and the earth. I love that Moses took off his shoes to start the journey that would carry him through forty years in the desert and to Mount Nebo, where he would lay down and be at rest. I love that we can follow in his footsteps and remember the holy ground that we are walking on and tending. I love that this whole world is holy, and part of our journey is to remember our place in the tabernacle of creation.

QUESTIONS FOR REFLECTION

1. What "barefoot" practices might allow you to be more discerning in your life's journey?

2. What footprints do you make for others to follow?

The Fellowship of Farming
From Outside of Kampala, Uganda

⤺ We know love by this, that he laid down his life for us—and we ought to lay down our lives for one another.

1 JOHN 3:16

She came running up to me, a stranger, asking if I could help her raise some money. She told me that people had said that if she could find me, I could help her get funding for her project. I almost told her I was too busy to help when I realized I was already asking questions about her work and finding myself engrossed in her farming project. Her knowledge of the land, her ideas for social enterprise and feeding programs in Kampala . . . all were very compelling. She was a master farmer and really just needed some good old-fashioned fellowship, networking, and support to take it up a notch. She didn't need my advice; she didn't need me to give her another idea. She needed a friend with some resources in the hard work of justice farming. Farmers are friends who understand the daily hard work and the need, every now and then, to have someone else look at what you have accomplished and say, "Great job. You have done amazing work."

This is especially true in the fields of justice. Often, looking for a bit of fellowship and funding, what you find are people who want to give you advice and critique your project. One of my favorites is the "O" word. It's the part of the conversation when you have talked about your work and the need for more funding when someone says, "You should go on Oprah." "Thank you," I say as I think to myself, "Do you honestly think we never wanted to go on the Oprah show?" It was somewhat of a relief when that show ended, partly because I knew that now people would just say, "You need to get a celebrity to endorse the Thistle Farms products." For now, though, I could see myself in this Ugandan farmer, working for a farm-to-table system. She knew the issues and how to do the work better than any of us outsiders she was hoping to "cultivate." I asked if it would be possible for me to tour her farm and shops to see some of the innovative water filters and briquettes her team was manufacturing.

This letter is a plea to fellow farmers in the work of justice. Ready your own wallets for a friend and reduce the unsolicited critique that forms in the back of your head. It's hard to be just a friend and supporter, but that is one of the most desperately needed commodities in this work. I wish more workers saw the fields of justice as noncompetitive and joined together as friends to support one another. There is a unique blessing in sharing, even when our own resources feel tight, to pull and cheer for one another—even asking on behalf of another and not just for your own small farm.

I was amazed by what I saw when I visited this brilliant Ugandan farmer. She was a gifted entrepreneur, loved the land, knew the names of all the birds and wildflowers we saw along our journey the next day. At the end of that day she showed me an album of the places she has been and the people she had met. I offered her what I had and we became friends that day. I learned from her and felt the joy of kinship. We need so much more fellowship and so much less competition.

On my return to the United States, I gave a presentation at a university during which a student asked me about a new tea venture Thistle Farms had formed in Uganda. The question was, "Who is your biggest competitor?" My answer was that I am done with competition, especially since our so-called biggest competitor probably doesn't even know I am alive. Instead, I am looking for my biggest allies who can join with us and be in fellowship. Everyone in the work of justice needs more friends, not a clearer picture of competitors. We can find spiritual renewal in this work through silence, music, prayer, and reading. One of the best and most treasured ways, though, is to find a new friend and to commit to being in fellowship and support of each other's farms. Love and love.

QUESTIONS FOR REFLECTION

1. Is it difficult for you to be generous to colleagues or neighbors?
2. Who could you view as your ally and colleague rather than your competitor?

Be a Bold Farmer

At David Lipscomb University,
Nashville, Tennessee,
Talking to Business Students

～ Now faith is the assurance of things hoped for, the conviction of things not seen.

HEBREWS 11:1

This may be the most businesslike letter I write. I am writing to those in leadership positions within churches and other not-for-profit organizations with the hope that this letter can support a leadership that is imbued with imagination, humility, and courage. Leadership marked by boldness has seven facets that help define it. Moreover, this leadership is colored by a confidence in daily tasks and a trust in the leaps of faith that define the nature of justice work.

1. Leadership that trusts the Spirit moving. Private prayer practices and faithful walks will help develop awareness of the Spirit. Since the beginning of Thistle Farms, I have learned to trust that the Spirit moves in the community through my own imagination, through the words of others, and from times of discomfort and stress. The Spirit can move freely when we are a little off our game, feeling vulnerable, and focused on the issues of justice and the well-being of others.

2. Leadership that practices generosity in ideas and in giving credit. "Great job" is a phrase we need to practice with our coworkers, congregants, board members, and fellow pilgrims.

All of us have great ideas and all of us have ideas that flop. It helps the cause to give credit to others, to be generous in our mindset, and to live in the truth that the Spirit moves through us all.

3. Leadership that doesn't live in the box. You cannot think outside the box if you are always living in the box. Allow yourself to step out of the box so that you can think from there. That may mean a change of scenery, a change of mind such that you do not define yourself by your family or work status, or a change of heart in which you focus on empathy for the one deemed least among us. It is from this place that new models for informing business and community can most easily be born. It is from this place that we can think radically about the deepest things we believe and about our highest ideals.

4. Leadership that takes things once pitted against each other and turns them into partners. In the work of church and charity the word "competition" needs to be replaced by "cooperation" at every turn. There is plenty of work and what we need are partners and friends to help us lead.

5. Leadership that speaks truth even through a shaking voice. Boldness does not mean that we don't feel fear or don't worry about the repercussions of our words. It means that we know we are speaking our truth in love and that it is more important for us to speak than to keep silent. When we feel called to preach or teach, we trust our words will have an impact on the communities we serve. Accordingly, we are obliged to voice our thoughts. There are definitely times for silence and times to hold our tongues, but there are also times to speak as we work toward a more loving and just way of being together.

6. Leadership that keeps growing and developing. Over the last twenty years I have become less interested in leadership types and much more interested in the leadership spirit. The spirit I am most drawn to is one that remembers we are all students on the spiritual journey, with much to still learn and more to forgive and be forgiven for.

7. Leadership that comes at a cost. There is always a price for taking leadership and bold leaders are aware of that. They are not afraid to accept the loss of freedom and privacy for the positions they take. It is a great gift to be given authority within a community and to lead well. We need to offer up our lives for the sake of others.

QUESTIONS FOR REFLECTION

1. Which of these seven facets of boldness is the greatest challenge for you?
2. Among the qualities of imagination, humility, and courage, which do you bring to the challenge?

Remember the World
Is Our Farm

From the Side of the Road
in Burns, Tennessee

～ I looked, and there were four wheels beside the cherubim, one beside each cherub; and the appearance of the wheels was like gleaming beryl. And as for their appearance, the four looked alike, something like a wheel within a wheel.

EZEKIEL 10:9–10

～ Where can I go from your spirit? Or where can I flee from your presence? If I ascend to heaven, you are there; if I make my bed in Sheol, you are there. If I take the wings of the morning and settle at the farthest limits of the sea, even there your hand shall lead me, and your right hand shall hold me fast.

PSALM 139:7–10

I hope this letter finds its way into a seminary where a young idealist wonders if it is possible to live into their best hopes for this world. I can still remember sitting in seminary and wondering how I could live into what I understood were the ideals of the gospel. I felt inspired through teachers and texts to be uncompromising in my goals, but I was also pretty limited in my vision and needed to grow into the idea that all visions are global, even when they come to us individually.

Ezekiel could see a wheel in a wheel in a cloudy sky one day near his home. It was probably the same sky he had looked into for years, but on one particular day with the sun in a particular arc with his heart particularly open, he saw a wheel in a wheel. It was a simple and particular vision, but what it preaches is universal and can still be seen today. Sitting in a lavender field in Burns, Tennessee, thousands of years later, I can just about capture that vision as I gaze into dreamy clouds that look like wheels in wheels. As I stare into the clouds, I imagine a woman working on the same day on a Rwandan farm looking up and sharing the same vision as she finishes harvesting a sack of geranium. I wonder if my mom and her mom saw similar clouds as they gazed up from their dairy farms one day and glimpsed at wheels in wheels like Ezekiel. They are not that hard to see. If you can see dragons and ships in clouds, finding a wheel in the middle of the sky is possible.

Over and over, one person's simple vision is translated over time and distance and the universality of what we are seeing and believing is shared. It makes sense to me now that a small idea about sanctuary in Nashville would blossom into a whole community envisioning healing the wider world. The wheel in the wheel in Nashville that offered healing and hope to survivors was seen in manifold skies across the United States and slowly but surely more than twenty sister communities have begun with a similar vision of sanctuary.

As Thistle Farms began to grow, our vision of how love heals needed to grow with the work. We learned that visions need to be global in order to help individual women feel freedom. We needed to imagine a global farm big enough to reach a poor grandmother in Mexico who has never had a home, and a young woman in Uganda who is just learning she can name her pastor as her abuser. If we want our faith to be rooted in love and grown organically, we need to think about the whole world as our farm. That is a big farm.

The roots of that goal started small, and the universal farm has taken almost two decades to cultivate. When we began, it was simply a small house and five women. We developed the model for sanctuary from our deepest desire—to believe that love is strong enough to heal us and change the world. The whole endeavor to create safe community, though, probably began about twenty-five years before, after my experiences of childhood trauma, including the death of my father and the ensuing sexual abuse. The nature of the community we formed was rooted in my own fears about the potential for abuse in the institutional church and in my hope that together we can learn to love without judgment. I needed the community of Thistle Farms as much as the women coming off the streets needed the community. We all need to feel that love heals.

I remember a day standing in a field by the highway. Seeing a half-dead field of thistles as a lavish harvest, I knew that by God's grace I had stumbled upon my life's calling. I had been searching for thistles to make products and, as I looked out into the field that most people would view as ugly and useless, I thought, "I am a thistle farmer." Standing among the field of thistle, I felt I was offered a vision into my own brokenness, my troubled past and all the mercy offered me by others. I swear if I had thought to look up, I would have seen a wheel in a wheel in the middle of that field. Never giving up on our ability to love with power had offered me the gift of standing in a huge field of weeds, and feeling like I was imbibing a rich promise. Being a thistle farmer is a way of walking into the troubled fields of the world. As a thistle farmer, I find that the world becomes a plentiful field with no borders, owners, or strangers; a place where everything can be used for healing. Anyone can harvest thistles, and when you can see the beauty and value of the thistle, it is easy to remember that there is nothing in all of creation left to be condemned.

The vision of healing is global and there is nowhere we can flee from the Spirit of God. We can see the wheel in the wheel way up in the middle of the air from the sea, from our own pits of despair, and from the lofty mountains. The vision of God's healing surrounds us and hems us in like the air itself. Whether or not we feel it, can see it, or even hope for it, it is there. Visions and thistles are universal and particular. They are as varied as your thumbprint, a unique impression that marks you as a loving member of the family farm.

QUESTIONS FOR REFLECTION

1. What visions have you had for your life?
2. How have those visions been interrupted or stalled or brought to fruition?

Cultivate the Tender Soil
of Forgiveness
Austin, Texas

Then Peter came and said to him, "Lord, if another member of the church sins against me, how often should I forgive? As many as seven times?" Jesus said to him, "Not seven times, but, I tell you, seventy-seven times."

MATTHEW 18:21–22

My hope is that this letter finds its way to someone who wants to learn how to forgive. It could be a survivor of abuse or any seeker who has yet to believe they can find some path of peace. I have been married to Marcus for more than twenty-five years and I think I have forgiven him about seventy-two times—our three boys, maybe closer to seventy-five. What I would hate to do though is count how often they have forgiven me. It has to be in the hundreds, if not thousands, and that is without including the untold number of times I have been forgiven by the communities around me in which I work. There is no way to count sins of omission or commission, things done and things left undone. The things we harbor in our hearts and the things we do in oblivion, addiction, laziness, or selfishness. There is a reason there are a variety of confessions of sin in the prayer book for our regular use. None of us can keep a tally of forgiveness. When we think of forgiveness, we usually begin by trying to imagine how we could possibly forgive someone else, but if we begin by remembering how much we have been forgiven, it seems possible. Jesus knew a tally of forgiveness was impossible in community.

In this passage from Matthew we see the community trying to figure out how to grow and live into the possibility of forgiveness. Jesus reminds the disciples that the Spirit of God dwells with them and what they bind on earth is bound in heaven and what they release on earth is released in heaven. Peter asks, "How many times do I have to forgive?" The answer is, "More than you can count," and the parable gives a vivid image of how deplorable it is for us to be an unforgiving people. The parable asks us to consider who we think we are, given all we have been forgiven, that we cannot forgive our brothers. Jesus lives into this ideal of forgiveness so passionately that even in the end, hanging on a cross, he asks for forgiveness for his torturers. "Forgive them, for they do not know what they do."

Forgiveness happens in the aftermath: the place we find ourselves dwelling in after the tally can't be reckoned, when the list of whom we have harmed or been harmed by is overwhelming, when we can no longer bear the weight of a broken heart. Too often fear or resentment creeps into our lives and hardens us, making a path toward forgiveness impassable. That's when we feel like taking the soil from which we are made and fire it into bricks to build a wall around our hearts. Forgiveness allows us to feel the swords that would divide us actually turn into ploughs that can cut through hard and rocky soil . . . soil we thought could never grow seeds of love again. We use a plough made from beating our own anxiety and frustrations into compassion for others and their suffering. The plough is driven by hard work, a desire to be free, and by remembering all we have been forgiven. I long for this plough to cut through the pain we hold onto like a fallow, untouchable field.

Forgiveness doesn't try to skip over hard earth. It calls us to dig deep into that soil and find ourselves knee-bucklingly deep in the mangled earth of truth. It doesn't ask us to pretend an act never happened, but to engage the person behind the act in a way that offers a path where forgiveness is possible. That path is carved with our own sweat and tears from the hard work. In that soil we find the holy seedling of forgiveness taking root and tender shoots of hope rising. Forgiveness is surely the highest virtue and the miracle of faith. To forgive someone removes their hold on our lives and allows us to walk freely along the path we have made.

I was sitting with Ty this summer as she spoke to a group in Texas about her life and recovery. Ty, a candle maker at Thistle Farms, graduated from our two-year residential program. She began her story on that Texas afternoon by remembering the early abuse, the hard drugs, and the rough road. Through it all she exuded an amazing compassion that filled the air with a scent as tangible as the geranium oils we were hawking on the side. After Ty came to Magdalene, there was still one more warrant to be served on her from a small town outside of Nashville. After a year of living clean and sober, following the twelve-step path of recovery from addiction, prostitution, and trauma, she was rearrested, sentenced, and sent to the Tennessee state prison for women. For more than three years she sat there waiting out her sentence. For just about as long as most folks go to college, she sat there, waiting and waiting to return home. I marvel at Ty, I marvel at her ability to forgive it all and exude gratitude where bitterness could have easily taken root. She could have taken up a sword to fight the injustices of a system that never took into account the rapes she endured in her bedroom closet before her twelfth birthday, the institutional poverty and racism that affected the outcome of her trial, or the wasted years she could have been working at Thistle Farms and making money. If you ask her, "How did you do it? How did you forgive it all?" she says with a genuine lilt in her voice, "Community. This was the only time I went to prison and wasn't on my own. None of my sisters, especially Shelia, abandoned me. I could take it all, because they loved me, they wrote letters, they came to see me, they put money on the commissary card, and they promised they would be there when I got home. I was grateful."

Together, we beat our swords into ploughshares in gratitude. In Paul's letter to his community in Rome we learn first to be grateful for all the mercy; the next step is to learn how to love without judgment. Hard hearts cannot soften another's. Only hearts that are exuding love without judgment can offer that gift. Paul reminds us in the fourth chapter of the book of Romans that the act of forgiving requires that we do not judge. "Don't judge anyone," he implores them, "for God has welcomed them."

This is a central teaching of every religion. Buddhism teaches us that hatred of another never ceases by hatred, but only by love. Martin Luther King, Mahatma Gandhi, and countless other tillers of tender and forgiving soil speak only of love in the midst of hate, tenderness in the face of fear, and compassion in the work of justice. This may be the simplest and deepest thought given to humanity—and the least practiced. To grow a faith requires a heart of flesh that loves without judgment and forgives generously.

When we use this plough of forgiveness and love without judgment, we dig deep and find new springs and visions that had been covered with dry, barren soil. This freshly turned and fertile soil of our hearts is rich enough to plant the seeds of forgiveness by word and example for all those ready to maybe, just maybe, return to the path of freedom and peace.

QUESTIONS FOR REFLECTION

1. Can you think back, not on your whole life, but on the last week and recount all the forgiveness you have been offered or offered another?

2. What freedom was found in that tender soil?

Cultivating Peace
From a Tea Estate in South Carolina

For you shall go out in joy, and be led back in peace; the mountains and the hills before you shall burst into song, and all the trees of the field shall clap their hands. Instead of the thorn shall come up the cypress; instead of the brier shall come up the myrtle; and it shall be to the Lord for a memorial, for an everlasting sign that shall not be cut off.

ISAIAH 55:12–13

May this small letter be a prayer for the wanderers who have not yet found peace in the wild fields. I have spent the better part of my ministry seeking to understand the great spiritual gifts offered through plants and the rest of creation, immersing my work and community in that knowledge.

I have spent years as director of Thistle Farms learning how to cultivate herbs for distillation, finding the best essential oils from around the globe, and opening a café that serves special tinctures of herbal teas. I have done some of it peacefully, but way too much of it stressed about money, deadlines, and family. I have written books on the healing power of essential oils and the way tea can offer justice and healing for women in the world. But many times I gulp down those "peaceful" cups of tea while answering e-mails. Writing about it for others and trying to live by it are two very different things. My writing about peace means that I probably still long for it. Someone once told me that preachers preach what they most need to hear. My guess is that all of us present our lives in public with some care, and beneath that facade hide secret habits, fears, and coping skills that we keep to ourselves and perhaps the few people who know us best. The goal is not to pretend that divide doesn't exist, but to have those two parts in conversation with one another so they live closer together and we can feel more peaceful.

Those two parts of my life came together walking through a tea field.

Thistle Farms was just beginning to expand into the tea industry. It was important to go to the only working tea farm in the United States, in South Carolina, as we decided if we should import or start our own tea farm. The sun was at the apex of its trajectory as it scorched the July day. Weeds were thriving alongside the tea plants; the bugs were so thick they looked like sprinkles on hot doughnuts. I felt the need for water, shelter, and community as thick as the air that hugged my lungs. But there was a peace as I walked alone among the weeds and tea plants.

Tea is the oldest cultivated plant in the world, requiring little tending. Tea is not bothered by sharing the field with pesky weeds and so it all mingles among a variety of plants in this rich land known to produce thirtyfold a season. There were no pickers out in the field at this hour, no tourists, and, thank God, no cell phone coverage. The sound of bugs became white noise as the peacefulness of the field filled me with the hope that one day I might truly be a farmer who knows peace. It wasn't about understanding, but about acceptance. I could imagine all the farmers throughout the state of South Carolina wiping their brows and sitting under trees for shade. I could imagine the farmers out west teaching the next generation about walking among the rows and identifying varieties in plants. I almost could see small rice paddies and coffee farms owned by small farmers in distant lands. Can we learn to live like farmers, whether we are digging up dirt or walking through the world harvesting hope? To be willing to be in thick, hot air and sweat and toil without stressing about the overwhelming noise filling us. We can't intellectualize our way to peace—instead we seek it, we sit in it, and we find it unexpectedly in field and farms where creation is allowed to preach.

QUESTIONS FOR REFLECTION

1. What aspects of your life and faith exist in tension with each other?
2. Where do you seek peace?

Grow Tree Roots
In the Healing Garden at Thistle Farms

⟋‿‿‿ It is the smallest of all the seeds, but when it has grown it is the greatest of shrubs and becomes a tree, so that the birds of the air come and make nests in its branches.

MATTHEW 13:32

In our small healing garden at Thistle Farms we planted an old school chestnut tree four years ago. It's not the newer Chinese chestnut variety, but a variety created by botanists over many years, carefully engineering the old American chestnut to withstand the blight that wiped out about 4 billion trees in the early 1900s. We were thrilled that a nursery in North Carolina had entrusted us to tend the tree and waited expectantly for this great sign of new life. When it came it was a small twig about two-and-a-half inches tall. "That's it?" I asked, a bit deflated. It seemed incomprehensible to me that this tiny stick was going to live at all, let alone withstand a horrible blight inherent in the American chestnut. Nonetheless, we took it from the tin can it arrived in and placed it in the ground as instructed by the growers. We built a little safety net around it so that no one would step on it by accident. We watered according to directions. It didn't change for a year.

All the other native Tennessee plants around the chestnut blossomed and offered stunning foliage over that summer, but this chopstick of a plant just sat there. Finally the next spring the tiniest bud appeared. There were only a handful of leaves. The next year was marked by substantial growth; it stood almost twelve inches high with tiny limbs and probably twenty leaves. Again the seasons came around and the next spring more growth, more leaves. We finally had a true sapling.

This year it stands waist high with broad branches, looking like the pictures of actual chestnut trees in the books I have read. You can begin to imagine the magnificence of its future and the deep roots carving new paths in secret. It has been with us for four years and it is finally coming into its own. What I have learned from this tiny, amazing tree could fill its own book. It has taught me that new ideas can be small and fragile and yet grow into something beautiful, provided a caring environment and patient hearts. Too many times we start with huge ideas that never take root. Sowing seeds of recovery and raising branches of justice begin with fragile hopes that need to be tended with gentle actions.

The second lesson from the tree is that grass roots are not always synonymous with movements. I hear the word "movement" tossed around a lot. Often the term is used in reference to a campaign to buy T-shirts, sign up online, or donate money to a cause. Those are all great things, but they are not movements. A movement is bigger than all of that. It is deeper and wider and demands that we offer a significant amount of our time, talent, and treasure to its growth and development. Movements are really not grass roots, they are more like tree roots that push deep and wide, allowing an idea or plant to grow big and strong and shape the landscape around it.

Growing deep roots takes years. It's more than laying sod and watching the grass grow. It's committing ourselves to place and time enough to see the wonder of steady growth.

The third lesson is that real growth isn't always visible to the naked eye. There is work going on below the surface; time on the farm is measured in seasons, not days. We long to see things get better and outcomes are a driving force in the world of fundraising. But how do we measure healing? How do we quantify joy taking root in a fellow traveler as they live in a loving community? How do we know if all the work is making a difference? The answer is, "Thank God we can't." We can only tend with faithfulness and water the plants around us. We cannot sufficiently discern healing and joy. We do not always know the outcome. Tending the farm doesn't offer us complete assurance, instead it offers us wonder and the deepest desires of our hearts.

QUESTIONS FOR REFLECTION

1. What fragile hopes have you had in your life that grew, over time, into fruition?

2. What actions, on your part or on the part of others, nurtured and sustained those hopes?

Weep at Injustice
Kampala, Uganda

⟡ He said, "Where have you laid him?" They said to him, "Lord, come and see." Jesus began to weep.
JOHN 11:34–35

This letter is intended for the tenderhearted. Those who still weep unashamedly at the injustices in this world are, in fact, looking at the world through a lens of compassion. This world needs more compassionate hearts, just as a farm needs water in a drought. The power of compassion and courage is a beatific mystery as deep as the possibility of the meek inheriting the whole world. When we encounter strangers' stories that tap into our hearts, acknowledging the injustice that has shortened so many lives, it is right that the wellsprings of our hearts open, offering saltwater signs of solidarity.

This summer I was driving down a dirt road in Uganda with Canon Gideon, the founding director of Hope University, which helps survivors of HIV/AIDS and vulnerable youth in Uganda. He has been a dedicated worker, advocating for decades for access to medical care, a nonjudgmental church, and streams of income for children who have lost their parents to AIDS. We were talking about working with women who have known the underside of bridges, the backside of anger, the inside of prison walls, and the short side of justice. Our conversation meandered as freely as the back roads we were traversing. At one point I told Gideon the story of digging beneath the roots of my childhood sexual abuse as a woman in my early thirties and deciding to confront my abuser. I was surprised that the first question my abuser asked me was, "Who have you told?" In response, Gideon told me that when he was in seminary in 1988 and learned that he was HIV-positive, he went to tell the head of the seminary. He said he was shocked to hear his professor say, "Don't tell anyone." We talked about the fear of rejection and judgment that tells people who are survivors of violence and disease to keep our shame and brokenness hidden. If we thought that the response to our stories would be weeping at the hurt and fear, maybe more folks would share their story.

It is the people who want to oppress or maintain the dysfunction who will say, "Don't tell." My hope for both community and church is that as we hear hard stories, we don't say, "Keep it a secret." Instead, my hope is that we learn how powerful a healing tool it is to weep with one another . . . to weep at oppression and to stand with the brave men and women who fight for truth. We need more weepers who cry with protesters, who pray with those in the midst of the ravages of war, and who feel the hunger with children who are growing up in the bosom of institutional poverty.

After Gideon and I bonded in our mutual compassion club, he shifted the conversation to the patriarchal system in Uganda that allows culturally acceptable forms of violence through oppressive laws and systems. Gideon combats these not only by fighting the laws in the courts and legislature, but also by poking holes into the very fabric of the unjust cultural norms people so often accept. As he talked, driving along a bumpy road, I thought about his work and ministry. He could leave. He has been honored with degrees from around the world and has friends in each of those places. He stays because he is a true farmer, a man dedicated to raising justice and loving the outcast. He stays because he is called to do this work that will cost him his whole life. Bumping along the outskirts of town, talking about civil disobedience against his government and his beautiful plans to raise a new school, I began to feel the outpouring of love in tears on my cheeks. I was moved by his passion, vision, and commitment. He is the preacher that reminds me today, as I head back into the fields that comprise this world, that love and faithfulness can be hard, costly, and lonely. In the midst of it all, however, his optimism is contagious and uplifting as he works to raise the funds that provide for hundreds of children.

Tears are signs of the Spirit moving in our lives. They are signs that we are moved and that we are humble enough to be vulnerable. I don't ever want to get to the place that I don't weep at injustices, at funerals, and anytime I feel the Spirit moving over us. Tears remind us that we are mortal, formed of dust and to dust we shall return. If heaven is the memory of God, when we weep over one another it is a kind of heaven on earth. The world can be a pretty harsh farm; I think it could use a bit more watering with our tears.

QUESTIONS FOR REFLECTION

1. What going on in the world today stirs you so deeply as to make you weepy?

2. When was the last time you offered tears of compassion for a fellow farmer?

Wild Fruits of the Spirit
Northern Michigan Woods

⟋⟍ What more was there to do for my vineyard that I have not done in it? When I expected it to yield grapes, why did it yield wild grapes?

ISAIAH 5:4

⟋⟍ The slaves said to him, "Then do you want us to go and gather [the weeds]?" But he replied, "No; for in gathering the weeds you would uproot the wheat along with them. Let both of them grow together until the harvest."

MATTHEW 13:28-30

In the wild place where wheat and weeds grow there is a tangle of plants that can teach us about our hearts. A deity visited the Buddha when he had first begun to teach, posing a question about the way people are caught up in inner and outer tangles. The deity asked, "What person can succeed in untangling this tangle?" The Buddha answered that the one who sits down in the middle of his or her life and looks with attention, calm and resolute, has a chance to untangle the knot and thereby relieve suffering.

So sitting in the wild woods in Canada, as a devotee of thistles, chickweed, and lupine, I offer this letter to anyone in a tangle—or in the blessed place of weeds. It comes from my love of the discipline and gift of cultivated fields, but also knowing the gift of weeds in my life, whether from neglect of those fields or from wandering into the unknown. It comes from a belief that love begets love.

There is something especially sweet about finding wild blueberries in the summer. It's like finding money on the sidewalk or seeing the first firefly of spring. It's actually better, because along with the surprise of the find, there is the instant gratification that immediately you can pop the delicious blueberries into your mouth. The blended color is a rich matte of purple and pinks. Yes, there are things like ticks and deer flies that require attention, but the joy of a handful of blueberries on a sunny afternoon hike surpasses the irritation of a few bugs or the trepidation of sitting on a garter snake. Blueberries are a feast that tastes like a foretaste of the heavenly banquet. Can you help but say grace as you pop the first one in your mouth and taste its real sweetness with a hint of a tartness to excite the palate?

Blueberries are found among the weeds in northern woods where moss and pines make paths like carpets and loons call people into the morning. Weeds grow freely in the wooded landscape, serving as ground cover and food. There were no weeds in a place called Eden. Everything grew together, blueberries and chickweed, living in harmony so both could prosper. Weeds were named as such by us, called out for their invasive nature and particular barbs. While we may label certain plants as weeds, tearing them out so that other plants can prosper, there is always a place for weeds. They protect as well as harm and hold many healing qualities within their leaves and flowers. There are even varieties known as nurse weeds that help other plants grow. There is a reason that wild blueberries are tucked among the weeds that protect them from insects and shield against harsh winds.

I have long held the view that since no plants were named as weeds in the vision at the beginning of creation, in the fullness of time when the kingdom of love is poured out, nothing will be categorized a "weed" again. We will have discovered that the healing presence lives in all things and removed the labels from any lush wild field where the river of life flows.

As Jesus walked toward Jerusalem over those three years, it is not hard to imagine the oppression and anger he faced in the midst of occupation. He saw the lepers, the women on the streets, the sick centurion's daughter, the woman bleeding, the blind man, and countless others suffering and deemed "weeds" by others. He witnessed firsthand the institutional sins of slavery and poverty, yoked in the desire for power. God who is merciful reminds us by allowing the weeds to grow that there is nothing we need to condemn and no one we need to leave behind. We cannot forsake those who are mourning or in prison. We cannot abandon anyone, whether they be Roman occupiers, the religious authority that conspires with them, or the rebels protesting against them. Let us all grow together; we are not here to judge. God will sort it out. It was a gift to those whom Jesus touched—and to us—to remember that there is a place for weeds and a place for each of us.

QUESTIONS FOR REFLECTION

1. What are the nurse weeds that have helped nurture you?
2. What have you learned from the weeds amid the wheat?

Don't Wait for Inspiration,
Be Reinspired as You Work
Burns, Tennessee

⌒‿ I will pour out my spirit on all flesh; your sons and daughters shall prophesy, your old men shall dream dreams, and your young men shall see visions.

JOEL 2:28

This letter is offered in praise for all the day laborers who are faithful to the ordinary tasks of loving their neighbors. Joel's prophesy of the young seeing visions and the old dreaming dreams happens naturally in the fields. It is in the work of monotonous toiling that you notice a hawk cut through an endless sky and feel inspired, noticing how quickly annoying headwinds become ecstasy with a graceful turn of wings. Digging into fresh soil and unearthing a worm becomes a metaphor for richness and new beginnings. Sensing bees nearby quickens the heart like a tiger in the woods to be silent and still, Buddhist fashion. Watching the arc of the sun allows the mind to drift through memories that sit like old wine on the back shelves of our hearts. There are visions and dreams rooted in our own hearts in the field. The daily work of tending those fields leaves room for wonder, fantasy, sadness, and new dreams.

The quotidian tasks of weeding, watering, and pruning are enough to grow new dreams. I have learned through the practice of daily disciplines that I am not always inspired to go out into the field. Yet in hours I spend doing the work of the field, I find myself inspired. In all our work, we can either burn out or be set aflame by the routine obligations that are ours.

Sometimes I feel so weary going to visit someone in prison, wondering how long I can continue to do the work. By the time I leave, though, I am energized and eager to challenge the system on behalf of the thousands and thousands of women in prisons and jails, the majority of whom experienced childhood trauma, including sexual and physical abuse. It doesn't matter if I feel inspired to go; inspiration will take care of itself. What matters is that I keep going. What matters is that I take into that prison new eyes that see the presence of God in the space and see visions of how we can all serve women better.

I used to imagine that I needed to go to the mountaintop to dream. I imagined that I would need to stand in front of a wondrous cave to hear the voice of God speak as Elijah did. But slowly I am learning that as I tend my children, work in the wild fields I have been given, and try to stay grounded, I can find new inspiration. The dreams and the work to inspire me are rooted right where I am. They grow in their practicality and their simplicity. I need not flee to find them. The beauty in a faraway lotus is no more profound than the discovery of the majesty of God's hand in the thistle growing right before me. There is nothing more sacred about the sparkle of a diamond than the sunlight and wind on the pond near my house. It's not always inspiring to do the work in our own backyard, day after day, year after year, but it is the place from which we grow our greatest hopes. It is the place where visions and dreams can flourish, if we pray to have the eyes and the ears to see and hear them.

I was working in a field weeding lavender, an endless job on an organic farm, when I heard a bird's song coming from a nearby tree. The bird was hidden, so I could only listen to its six-syllable mantra, over and over. At some point the song started to sound as if the bird was saying, "Listen, listen, listen." And so I started singing in my head as the bird chirped, "Listen, listen, listen." I wasn't even aware I was doing it. About forty-five minutes later, with a good sweat going and dirt firmly embedded under my nails, I realized I had been in something of an ecstatic trance for about twenty minutes. I could not have told you the time or a single thought I had. I was just listening and drifting, delighting in a vision and dream of oneness with the holy.

You can't buy that sort of experience; it comes as a gift as rare and priceless as the gilded chalice in an ancient cathedral. It comes naturally in the fields, simply in the doing. It reminds me that we are not always inspired to do the work of our vocations, but it is the work of our vocations that inspires us.

QUESTIONS FOR REFLECTION

1. When have you heard a calling that lightened your task or renewed your energy?

2. If you paused each day just to listen or reflect, what might you hear?

Be a Story-Keeper
Charlottesville, Virginia

⁓ For I tell you that many prophets and kings desired to see what you see, but did not see it, and to hear what you hear, but did not hear it.

LUKE 10:24

One of the great gifts of being a pastor is holding the stories of others in the role of confessor. We hold stories of those confessing in our hearts, not in our minds, remembering them differently and not as memorized details of stories we will recount one day. The stories we hear as pastors never leave our hearts. This letter is for all the faithful story-keepers: those who hold the rich dirt of whispered truths and carry those stories back to the earth. These are the holy stories we hold as sacred and swear never to share with another soul. People suffer from a lack of forgiveness and yet find there is no one in the whole world they trust to help them work through old shame or guilt. One of the greatest privileges is for someone to share their story with us, a privilege we hold as dear as a precious pearl found in a field, keeping it safe.

At the same time, though, it can be exhausting to listen, to be present and openhearted in our listening. Sometimes I forget that just listening to the story can be healing. This happened not too long ago on a flight. Usually when I fly I travel with women from Thistle Farms who have never flown before. It can be dramatic for them, yet it's an important part of growing a team of entrepreneurs, giving them new experiences and the confidence to sell our products around the globe. This flight to Virginia was different. I was flying by myself. The four women joining me for a national conference had arrived two days before. I wasn't looking after anyone, was not responsible for the person seated next to me, and was not going to have to be present. I could zone out with my crocheting and listening to the National Public Radio podcasts I had downloaded onto my phone.

As soon as I sat down, the young woman next to me said, "I'm so sorry, but I haven't flown before." I pretended that I had already turned on the podcast and didn't even respond. Then the agony of five minutes of guilt started building and I could feel my heart pressing against my chest and the conversation started in my head: How can I call myself a priest if I don't say something reassuring to her? When do I ever just get to "not care" for my neighbor, having no compassion on a stranger, and just not giving a damn? Maybe I don't care that she is going through a big event and is very nervous. After all, it is part of growing up: I had to go through it. Maybe she will never find out that I am a priest.

Thank God it didn't take me longer than the length of the runway to come to myself. The skill I learned in pastoral care 101 and have honed over decades is that I can hear her story as she pours it out. I don't have to do anything else. I can just be her story-keeper and listen as she tells me her fear and worry. More than likely I will never see her again in this world. It is nothing for me to do this, and it may be a gift to her to get through this flight. I told her what was going to happen as the plane took off, assured her that it would be fine, and gave her my headphones. It was her grateful tears that humbled me. Then she began to pour out the story of flying to see her husband, showed me the picture of her two small children, and unfolded a pretty sweet and sad story of her rural Tennessee life. She got pregnant young and, until this flight, had never left home. She is going back to school and she hasn't seen her husband, who served two tours of duty in Iraq and has never met his younger child. I am reminded that my perceptions of my time and my day off are trivial in a world where what matters is loving each other and listening to another's story. She can keep my stupid headphones if it gets her through the next leg of her flight. This young woman next to me is a great teacher. She reminds me to get out of my head when I am in the clouds and listen.

If we want to be farmers, helping the world to be a place where love and justice grow, compassion is the path. Compassion is the path on which we listen and hold stories. We are farmers, the world is our farm, and the people we encounter are essential to the love we hope to grow.

QUESTIONS FOR REFLECTION

1. Who has held your sacred stories for you?
2. Who might be waiting to tell you their story?

Find Joy in Your Work
On a Rented Farm, Presiding at a Wedding

Therefore my heart is glad, and my soul rejoices; my body also rests secure.

PSALM 16:9

People bring their extra vegetables to us at Thistle Farms. As a result, we are overrun by the end of summer with okra. People love to grow it, but eat it—not so much. This past summer a couple of women farmers brought in a clear plastic sack with more than two hundred pods of okra. They both tried to give the staff a great sales pitch for the okra. "It freezes great," one of the women said. The other said it was great for pickling. They wanted us to appreciate the gift, but in the back of my mind I thought, "So you couldn't find someone else to take it?" I thanked them both for their okra and for the far smaller amounts of squash and tomatoes they had also dropped off. I couldn't think of how in the world we were going to consume all that okra. But worrying about the bounty of a vegetable you aren't eager to eat is not the key to happy farming. The key to happy farming is learning to enjoy something about the okra that has become a mainstay of our donations each late summer at Thistle Farms. One of the women who works at Thistle Farms has recently acquired a deep fat fryer. We have started frying the okra in true southern fashion and have come to learn that fried and dipped in ketchup is a great way to get a group to consume about fifty spears of okra in one sitting!

This letter is offered as a reminder to find the joy in whatever is the okra of your harvest. The okra in the world of pastoring for me is weddings. I love many of the weddings at which I preside, but there have been just as many that were a huge time commitment and overly stressful. There have been a few that seemed an extraordinary waste of money or an occasion that was more of a fashion scene than religious rite. These are times I felt lonely and uncomfortable.

The problem with weddings is that some folks forget that the wedding is just the first thirty minutes of a marriage, a ceremony hijacked by an industry boasting billions in extravagances. There have been times when my reaction to an invitation to preside at a wedding was only that it would be another Saturday that I missed my sons' games or a chance to go hiking. That attitude neither honored the bride or groom nor helped me live in joy. So I changed. I started living into the truth that we can find joy in all our work. It wasn't that I made a resolution, I just surrendered to the truth that joy is found when we come grateful to the party. I started using the premarital counseling sessions more wisely, speaking about ritual in marriage *after* the wedding and using engagements as times of discernment. I started doing more weddings for couples who used the celebration to give gifts for others, who volunteered during their honeymoons, whose gift registry was on behalf of a charitable organization. One couple took the money for an engagement ring and gave it all away. When they told me what they had done, I was humbled and knew in my heart that they were going to have a happy marriage. All these efforts changed how I felt about the "wedding okra" of my farm and allowed me to discover a way to prepare it so that I neither wasted it, nor dreaded it.

For there to be joy in our hearts, we need to change. We want to be able to say grace over all our food, the okra and the tomato alike. We have to feel grateful for the work of weddings, for the parts of our jobs that are not on our wish lists and the tasks that drive us crazy. It is in all these things that we are nurturing a creative spirit that can be a source of joy and wonder. We want to have that joy, joy, joy, joy, down in our hearts. When we pray over a meal, we give thanks for all the food. When we bless a wedding, it is not just some couples that are blessed. To be a part of that thanksgiving and that blessing, it is our hearts that have to be open.

QUESTIONS FOR REFLECTION

1. What gifts are hard for you to receive?
2. What worn-out pattern in your life might be calling for your attention?

Digging for Our Own Healing
South Cumberland Plateau, Tennessee

⌒‿ So I say to you, Ask, and it will be given you; search, and you will find; knock, and the door will be opened for you.

LUKE 11:9

As I hiked through the woods in the South Cumberland Plateau, I found myself looking for yellow root. I kept thinking about how yellow root, the wild herb gathered for use in folk medicine—for sore throat, during childbirth, and as an antibiotic—is so much like a treasure. It looks plain and simple, like a parsley growing humbly near the ground, but as you dig it up, a bright yellow root shines like the sun. As I dug around to find some to make a tea, I wondered why I was so focused, searching the forest floor for this one plant on this particular afternoon.

I have long held the opinion that we are drawn toward our own healing. So if I was looking for yellow root, there was a good reason for it. After all, we named Thistle Farms after the weed to symbolize all that is cast aside, its beauty unrecognized, only to discover that thistle actually restores and detoxifies the liver. Since then I have felt the whole the community drawn to thistle. Women who have suffered from trauma and addiction need thistle to restore their balance and heal their livers. And so I have paid attention: one person loves the smell of the lavender candle while another swears by the tea tree. It has to do with what we long for and what we seek.

This letter is written as encouragement to remember what it is you are longing for, what it is you are seeking, and to take that longing into the woods to discover what draws you. Do you feel stirred by the sycamores? Swoon over larkspurs? How does honeysuckle or magnolia smell to you? And what does it mean about your need for healing—not a miracle cure, but the long and slow journey toward wholeness? We gratefully smell the lavender and remember we need peace. We touch a bergamot plant and feel a tiny muse enter our hearts. We dig up a yellow root and somehow feel comforted.

I went back to my church after the hike and looked up in my "big book" of healing herbs to find all the uses for yellow root. The reference I found said that yellow root can be used in teas to help some female conditions, especially at the beginning of peri-menopause. "Oh," I think to my humble self, "that makes sense to me." The feelings that have been waking me up before dawn, driving me to want to clean everything, and making me weepy at every worship service are indicators of a new stage of my life's journey. I want to welcome it, just as I tried to welcome the beginning of nursing and the end of childbearing. It made me grateful to know of yellow root and that something deep inside me knew to dig it up and boil a bit of it for some comfort.

We can all dig toward our own healing. We can learn the names of the plants—and the people—we encounter, discovering which ones tug at our hearts, calling us to want to breathe them in and hold them close.

QUESTIONS FOR REFLECTION

1. Using all your senses, what do you associate with peacefulness or healing?

2. What do you seek to restore your sense of wholeness? Where might this seeking take you?

The Labyrinth of Farming

Walking the Labyrinth inside
Grace Cathedral in San Francisco

A voice cries out: "In the wilderness prepare the way of the Lord; make straight in the desert a highway for our God."

ISAIAH 40:3

I haven't gotten very far in this world. I work about four miles from where I grew up. That doesn't mean that I haven't traveled far, physically or in my spirit. It just means that I have kept my "home altar" close and still need to stay close to the community I knew as a child. Most of us, in the circling we do throughout our lives, are given the opportunity to explore more closely the things that we passed by the first time around. Going up and down the same streets or rows does not have to put us in a rut. Instead, it can awaken our spirits as we notice more of the beauty of spider webs, cracks in sidewalks, new growth on a bud of a tree. I wrote a Bible study on just this topic ("Walking in Circles"). We walk in circles because it brings us awareness, allowing us to focus on the journey more than the destination and offering the opportunity to travel inward as we walk the same path over and over. The nature of farming and all spiritual paths is to walk with intention, remembering that we will end up pretty close to where we started: naked and in the arms of a loving God.

Flying over Nebraska you can see the huge crop circles that have taken the place of the outdated farming square, allowing for more efficient watering. From the clouds those three-quarter-acre farming circles look like giant labyrinths. Labyrinths are not mazes, nor are they puzzles. They are intricate paths that we walk with the intention of emptying ourselves of all that causes us harm to then refill ourselves with loving intentions for ourselves and the world. The history of sacred labyrinths dates back to the fourth century BCE, and while farming is almost ten thousand years older than that, both ancient practices have carried men and women through many literal and spiritual generations. One of the most famous labyrinths in the United States is housed in Grace Cathedral in San Francisco. When you walk this circular path your footsteps echo in the huge marble nave so you walk as quietly as possible. In that circle great prayers have been offered and countless miles have been traversed. As I move around the circle, it comes to my mind that the labyrinth is a great symbol for farmer disciples. In my own circling of the globe, I am learning to trust that I can travel lighter, than when I started, knowing I will come home. There is a freedom to walking and farming in a labyrinth pattern. Going up and down rows and covering a plot of land as carefully as possible, ending up at the end of a hard day of labor back where we started. It is easy to see the practical side of this labyrinth and how it works in this world. It is harder to see that we—all of us—need to traverse carefully in our farming of the fields. Up and down the rows, inch by inch and row by row.

QUESTIONS FOR REFLECTION

1. What familiar path might you travel more slowly, more observantly?

2. In what ways are you being called to "circle back"?

You Are What You Grow
Memphis, Tennessee

⌒ But those who wait for the Lord shall renew their strength, they shall mount up with wings like eagles, they shall run and not be weary, they shall walk and not faint.

ISAIAH 40:31

We don't always pray what we believe; sometimes we pray what we hope to believe. This letter is a reminder that our lives become what we grow. In my life I have learned to plant and to pray love is the most powerful force for change in the world. I have tried to raise this belief daily in my work and prayer life. Because I have longed to believe that for so long, I am coming to believe it more and more. I have learned slowly but surely to believe that hearts don't break. They pour out like a flooded river forgetting her boundaries, upturning old oaks and turning fallow fields into ponds. Hearts pouring out flood us with tenderness and tears as their unstoppable force draws us in. When hearts pour out, it is possible to imagine that justice can follow in its wake.

Isaiah's heart did not break amidst the pain of banishment and the loss of his nation. Instead, in words and deeds, he poured out his heart to God for never abandoning the people. Isaiah reminds us even in our doubt, we can be faithful—even in our weariness, we can be strong. Isaiah's life is like a rushing river whose course carved its own path deeper and wider as the rains came.

Prophets and disciples pour their hearts out with an unwavering belief that this torrent of love is strong enough to change the world. Their meandering path from calling to vocation as a voice for love and justice may begin as winding as a river, but it makes its way toward stronger waters. Their witness to love itself is beyond measure, exposing the old stone bedrock of our hearts. The ancient and modern disciples open the flood gates of generosity, compassion, and tenderness so no one has to live in isolation, cynicism, or fear.

This story of love poured out like a river has continued down through the ages and remains the powerful calling of our lives. Martin Luther King Jr. practiced throughout his life the tremendous power of love. On the day before his assassination he spoke to a community in Tennessee of Amos's call for justice to roll down like waters and righteousness like a mighty stream. Then he told his audience that when God calls, we need to be with Amos and the prophets who speak faithfully of love and justice. Dr. King used the term *ahimsa*, made famous in the West by Gandhi during the movement to free India. The term means that within each of us there is a nonviolent soul force. *Ahimsa* is as old and deep as the waters running through this earth. It is the basis for the message of Jesus, the Buddha, and all the prophets. Love is a force as old as the earth and when it is poured out for the world, nothing can stop it.

The harsh realities and hurt imposed by violence, poverty, trafficking, racism, disease, and frailty cannot break hearts. I know love is stronger than that. When Thistle Farms started to make healing oils, we chose *ahimsa*, the soul force of love, as our first blend. We have tried to be a witness to love's force. There have been seasons when the creek bed was dry, but we went on faith that water was running somewhere. Other times we have witnessed love pouring like the glory of a rushing river. I now sit in our meditation circle at Thistle Farms and marvel at a room packed with folks from England, Iceland, Bolivia, Arkansas, Texas, Oklahoma, and Georgia. They have come to sit with us and hear our healing message of love. One woman said she drove from Kentucky for "a cup of coffee and a good word." People are thirsty for the waters pouring from the river of love where the promise of justice lives.

Let us pledge our whole lives to pouring our love out for the sake of the whole world. Not because we believe it, but because we want to become love and believe in its transformative power in this world. Growing powerful love is how we live into the truth of the prophecies of Isaiah, Martin, and the community of Thistle Farms. Let us pour out our love as we embark to spread this good news of *ahimsa*. We are living proof that the war on poverty and for freedom is still being waged in the name of love. We are a living testimony, as long as we keep preaching every day of our lives in our words and deeds that love is the most powerful force for social change in the world.

QUESTIONS FOR REFLECTION

1. Where does *ahimsa* flow within you?

2. What time of doubt in your life eventually brought you clarity and strength?

Whispered Prayers
Oklahoma City, Oklahoma

◟＿＿ Then deep from the earth you shall speak, from low in the dust your words shall come; your voice shall come from the ground like the voice of a ghost, and your speech shall whisper out of the dust.

ISAIAH 29:4

People usually read alone. Even if we join a book group, we usually bring our solitude of reading into the group and share insights that arose as the voice in our head allowed silent words to speak. Even as I type these words onto a page, there is a very quiet voice in my head reading along as words as close to what I feel are being typed. Reading and writing become a whisper sometimes; my inside voice. I wonder as I write this letter what the whispered voice will sound like to one who picks up this page and translates the silent voice from paper into their own inner voice. This reader/translator could be male or female, prisoner or free. I hope this letter feels like a whispered prayer quiet enough for your heart to hear.

It is the whispered voice we long to hear in the quiet of the night. Those whispers can carry us into the morning. When fears feel loud and shadows dance by moonlight, it is quiet whispers that silence us enough to sleep. Whispers are a means by which prayers rise seamlessly through the loud din of noise. They can be heard in the empty lots where houses once stood. They rise in memory from burial grounds and circle trees like an arctic stream. Whispers are the voices we use when we want to share something intimate and secretive. They are the confessions between God and us.

Standing in a dusty field on the Oklahoma landscape I believe you can hear the echo of prayers that have accompanied farms since the first seed was scattered and the first harvest gathered. Reverberating over the horizon dotted with trees and oil rigs are old prayers from Indian grounds and well-worn farms. When the railroad came through, when the Indians were displaced, when they discovered oil, and when the great dust bowl settled, deep prayers were planted in this sod. As I walk into this empty field with its historic markers, a rookery of ibis sitting nearby along a dry riverbed are turning whispered prayers into shouting. The cacophony of sound from the individual birdsongs coming together like a surging alleluia chorus. We find our ways to deserted farms and dry riverbeds to get quiet enough to hear our own thoughts. When we get quiet enough I swear we can hear the chorus of prayers once prayed. Those prayers linger over us like ozone and when we are silent, truly silent, we can hear them. In all our running around, in our struggle to tend the fields where we toil our whole lives, there are sweet whispers that mark the path of our hearts the whole way.

When Israel was exiled and dust filled the mouths and thoughts of the captives, Isaiah had a vision that their voices could rise like a whisper out of that very dust. Isaiah's vision is moving and wondrous. Beyond captivity, pain, or fear, we can still offer a whisper as light as a kite string to carry a hope to the highest mountain. Those prayers sometimes feel powerless and wan, but truly they are light and strong enough to take flight. The more hefty prayers, offered before crowds and recited in unison, may be too heavy to make the trip from exile all the way to Sinai. We get to pray our hearts and we whisper our hearts to the heavens. We get to join with thousands of other prayer whisperers as our rookery becomes a din of hope rising from the dust. May we be silent enough to hear those whispers as we walk through this world, as we turn the pages of history, and as we travel to the depths of our own hearts.

1. What sacred or remembered place whispers to you?
2. Where has your inner voice found sanctuary or expression?

Find Ritual in the Mundane
London, England

◔──── I exhort the elders among you to tend the flock of God that is in your charge, exercising the oversight, not under compulsion but willingly, as God would have you do it.

1 PETER 5:1–2

It feels like we have been doing the same thing forever sometimes. My hope is that this letter is a balm to a soul toiling at the same tasks for years and ready for a reminder that the mundane tasks of watering and weeding are necessary so a great harvest can be reaped. For pastors, it's amazing how much of our daily work requires little of the skill sets we learned in seminary. It really has much more to do with being a faithful and good farmer who remembers to water and weed. I have been making posters, taking out the trash, and sitting through endless meetings for the duration of my work as a pastor. There is nothing wrong with any of it. When we can find ways to ritualize our daily routines, it allows us to find new meaning and joy in otherwise pretty boring work.

It is easy to walk into a cathedral in England and imagine the apostolic line of priests who have been doing the same work thousands of times and for eons. Imagining that reminds me that the work we do in pastoring congregations is good; not because it's that special, but because it is that sacred. It becomes a living prayer, rising from the tasks of loving others. Setting the altar, cleaning the linens, lighting the incense are fairly mindless tasks, but when we take the time to ritualize them, they become holy offerings that remind us that the sacred does lie in the mundane.

St. Benedict, the founder of a monastic order, felt that one of the great spiritual lessons was to keep the connections between the spiritual aspects of our lives and the daily tasks set before us. Ritualizing those tasks, in other words, making them a living prayer to be performed with intentionality, meant that we could live ordinary lives extraordinarily well. Ritualizing the task of doing dishes and setting the table can become opportunities to worship. Through this practice we make the present moment of how we are living holy. We find layers and layers of meaning as the endless days of tasks unfold and we dig deeper into the truth of being ordinary . . . and stunning people. I heard an old priest friend say once that, in addition to going to see a therapist, he recommends that people come weekly to clean the bathroom at the shelter he runs. He said that task helps so many people get to their knees and find new places in their hearts. Whether we pull weeds, wash dishes, or make body care products, it is holy as we remember we are in God's presence as we work at each task. We remember that we are loving our neighbors as best we can. We honor our families and remember those who performed those tasks from before we were born. The work we do is sacred; taking the time and intention to remember that fills us with new energy to do that work with a happy heart. I have always felt that hungry people do not care whether or not you are inspired to feed them. We just do the work, and do the work, and do the work, and find that through the great gift of that work, we have been inspired.

And so with a prayer of gratitude for all the shepherds of all the flocks in this world, I light a candle in the old cathedral and say a prayer of thanks. I am truly thankful to be in this endless line of work.

1. What daily tasks do you perform out of consideration for others in your life?

2. What new, simple, intentional steps could you take to bring ritual beauty to the mundane?

Old Ways, New Visions

⟜ The Spirit of the Lord is upon me, because he has anointed me to bring good news to the poor. He has sent me to proclaim release to the captives and recovery of sight to the blind, to let the oppressed go free, to proclaim the year of the Lord's favor.

LUKE 4:18–19

This letter is as close as I can find to a prayer for readers. It's a prayer to remember that most of our faith practices were a gift from older generations. The visions we see and the dreams we dream are formed in the context of old readings, old mountains, and old lore. On the farm, maybe more than any other venue on earth, we learn from those wiser. There is a sharing of wisdom and lore offered to those of us who are novices about what to plant and when; how to keep vermin out, how to space plants, and when to water. Farming may be a natural instinct but learning to grow plants is a gift from those willing to pass on the wisdom we are able to take to heart. We listen, we mimic, we absorb, and we improve our skills for the practice. It is especially true when you are using what you grow for healing. It is actually the "old wives' tales" that hold the truth about which plants can be used for which ailments. It was an eighty-year-old farmer who taught me how to make a tea from yellow root to heal a mouth sore. She had learned it from her grandmother, who collected yellow root in the spring when the kids didn't have enough vitamin C in their diets and were suffering. It was an old man down the street who taught me how to lay tobacco leaves on a sting to pull out the pain. It was my grandmother who taught my mom to give me cinnamon to feel better when I ached.

Would that we were so willing to learn from the old teachers concerning our faith! Instead of dismissing old practices like fasting, anointing, and meditation, what if we took them closer to heart? We could listen with an acute sense of the gift and take it to heart enough to practice the old skills. There is an art to practicing our faith just like practicing our farming and our cooking. It is a pilgrim's search for the heart. All the spiritual practices we cultivate are bound up in our longing to find communion with the eternal. We don't have to start from scratch. We can start with a deep pocket of knowledge offered to us by our forefathers and mothers who saw the same world and experienced the same longings.

Last night a group of thirty women gathered in my living room to talk about the history and purpose of the circle in our Magdalene community. The group was comprised of women survivors who have made their way from the streets and prisons into a healing circle where they have the time and space to find what they need to live into their sobriety. They held hands and wept in gratitude as we closed the evening. One woman said she was just ten days off the streets and, while she was completely lost still, she trusted that her sisters were going to show her the way. Then she said, "I have already learned that a grateful heart will keep me safe." Her tears were a symbol of all the gratitude for all the women who kept the circle going until she could make her way into the center of it. We do not always know how to live deeply into our faith; we do know that many others have kept the faith going until we could find our way into our own truth. Celebrate the old ways, celebrate the old saints, and then see what new visions and dreams arise.

QUESTIONS FOR REFLECTION

1. What wise lessons, gifts from those gone before, do you practice today?

2. Who are those who have "held the circle" for you, awaiting your arrival?

Communion Is for the Birds

The Yard of St. Augustine's Chapel
as Dawn Is Breaking

⟡ Even youths will faint and be weary, and the young will fall exhausted; but those who wait for the LORD shall renew their strength, they shall mount up with wings like eagles, they shall run and not be weary, they shall walk and not faint.

ISAIAH 40:30–31

Early this morning as the sun rose lazily, I went to pray for people in the community who were sick and suffering. My home altar is filled with incense stains and votive candle drippings from years of offered prayers. This particular morning I found that someone had left the remainder of a Eucharist on the altar, and I decided to step out to the yard to scatter the old bread crumbs. It seems these days that we are often too optimistic as we estimate how many folks might come to the Lord's Supper, so we keep consecrating too much bread.

The ritual of the Church is that after bread is consecrated it cannot be thrown away; it must be scattered over the earth or out to sea. It's nothing new to me to throw a bit of bread over the ground or cast my bread upon the waters. It's always been a sweet time as I imagine the animals feeding on it as they unwittingly take part in a Holy Communion. But today felt different in the dreary morning mist as the green of summer fades. The old field birds around the chapel were waiting for me with baited breath. They did not care about the liturgy or proclaiming, they wanted me to serve them. In this season of slim pickings, they were hungry to taste the body of Christ broken yesterday for the whole world. As I flung bits of a stale loaf out into the dry grass, I felt their hunger and was grateful to be their pastor. This Eucharist was for the birds. I could feel why Saint Francis preached to them and why Noah sent them out to find hope. I could feel their spirit picking up my mine and for a moment I was in communion with them. When I considered the birds of the air and the wild lilies of the field, I had no worries. I am so grateful for all the Holy Communions I have shared with all the creatures I have found to share a bite with me. I am grateful for the bounty of bread, slow mornings, and the willingness of birds to stop for a minute and bless my day. We are simply a part of creation hungry for love. Thank God for a bit of leftover bread and a flock of birds.

The birds of the air remind me that healing—especially that healing we find in the Eucharist—is not something that one person possesses and can "give" to another. It is a grace that washes over all of us, as we share our bread and our lives wherever we are and whoever we are with. Healing is sometimes a long walk, and sometimes it's just a moment of unbounded joy so powerful it sets us free.

QUESTIONS FOR REFLECTION

1. What in your life journey constrains you today?

2. What healing moments have aided you in moving through such constraints in the past?

We Are Tenants on the Farm
Villanova, Pennsylvania

⌇ Then [the landowner] leased [the vineyard] to tenants and went to another country. When the harvest time had come, he sent his slaves to the tenants to collect his produce.

MATTHEW 21:33B–34

It is a gift to remember that what we are farming is not ours and that we are to nurture our corner of the vineyard without thinking we own it. It reminds us that the work of faith is to be a part of a long and beautiful movement of loving the world as we make our way back to the land and the landowner. This letter is a simple invitation to anyone kind enough to read it to release what we might claim as ours and to be free to delight in tending the vineyard.

This passage from Matthew is heartbreaking when we look at the context. The mission is over for Jesus. He has entered Jerusalem on a donkey, cleansed the temple, and is now confronting the religious authorities who are trying to silence him without inciting the crowd. He will finish teaching these lessons in the temple, not victorious, but weeping over Jerusalem. This story in the larger context of the Gospel reminds us of the larger lesson of sacrifice and love Jesus preaches, even as he nears his own death. He continues to go toe-to-toe with those who can take his life, he continues to speak his truth, and he continues to love them with his whole heart. We are not the landowners: that's the lesson Jesus is preaching to those in authority and to all of us, desiring as we do to amass things that we claim as our own and defend to the death.

We are not the landowner who planted the vineyard and put a fence around it. We are not the one who dug a place for a winepress and built a watchtower. We are simply the tenants who have been gifted, living on the land and enjoying the harvest, as we serve our God for the sake of Love. In the end, all we can claim as ours is gratitude for what we had. It is the way to live peaceably, to abide in the commandments and to love our neighbors as our own. The landowner is the one who brought us out of Egypt. The landowner is the Holy One who created us, redeemed us, and loves us. The landowner is the one who reminds us that we are servants, committed to the way of life, not in control of it.

Sister Lucy was one of the most faithful tenants I have known. She was born on Monteagle Mountain, joined the order of St. Mary's, sang and played the guitar, led retreats like a zen master, and loved to laugh. She was not someone easily swayed. When Bishop Sanders was asked why, in 1981, he ordained her the first woman priest in the state of Tennessee, he simply said that if you were asking the question, you hadn't met her. She was a sister for more than fifty years and a priest for thirty-three years. She helped negotiate the land deal that established the retreat center at St. Mary's and raised funds to build the beautiful convent and chapel at Sewanee. For her whole life she helped sustain that community through her music and preaching, and she died without any assets or landholdings. She helped mentor and raise many children, and never claimed one as her own. In the end, all that we can claim as ours is gratitude for what we had.

At her funeral in the small chapel she helped to build, the container of her ashes rested near the altar on which a gold chalice had been placed. Sister Madeline, a dear friend and colleague of Sister Lucy's, reminded me before the service began that the chalice had been carried to Sewanee by the one surviving sister who had journeyed from Memphis to the mountaintop to start a new branch of the Order of St. Mary's. The Sisters of St. Mary's who lived in Memphis in the late 1800s had no training as nurses, but stepped up to care for the thousands who fell ill during the yellow fever outbreak. During the epidemic, more than fifty thousand people fled the city, as scared as the people in Guinea, Liberia, and Sierra Leone are today during the Ebola outbreak. Yet the sisters stayed. All but one of them died. They are known as the martyrs of Memphis. The one surviving nun, Sister Hughetta, moved to the mountain and carried the chalice as a reminder of the sacrifice the sisters made as they laid down their lives for the sake of love.

That chalice is a beautiful symbol of the meaning of the gospel: we are only tenants, and not landowners. The shiny, embossed chalice has been sitting on a plain wooden altar for more than one hundred years. In an otherwise simple chapel, it sparkles in the morning light as the sisters read psalms in slow unison. Those sisters are simply caretakers of the home they live in, the altar they worship before, and the cup they share. No one owns it or claims it as their own. They sip their whole lives from the cup until their spirits become part of the cloud of witnesses at the table and add to its value. At Sister Lucy's funeral, the chalice sat on the altar near her ashes as incense was presented before the altar and her ashes in a silent tribute. That incense gave depth to the light shining on both. The chapel was filled with light from huge bay windows overlooking the Cumberland Plateau. As the hills changed from green to dark blue in distant layers, people prayed and old bishops blessed. As I sat and marveled at the thick light, remembering what an incredible and faithful person Sister Lucy was, a small flock of birds flew by in a heavenly eulogy. Sister Lucy was just passing through this world as gracefully as the soaring arc of the birds. She has joined the communion of saints who, like all of humanity, move in and out, rising like incense with the prayers of all the faithful. Birds are beautiful preachers, flying above the fray, seeking freedom and carrying the graceful message that we are all simply "passing through." As I looked around at the humble gathering of friends and mourners, I realized that the whole service was almost a tearless occasion. It was filled with emotion, but Sister Lucy had made it so clear in her life that her commitment was to be a faithful tenant, her passing was as full of grace as it was sadness. May all of us be that faithful and clear about our commitment. May we live the rest of our days as faithful tenants who honor the landowner as we return to God.

QUESTIONS FOR REFLECTION

1. What (or who) have you claimed as your own that you might begin today to release?

2. For what have you been truly, abundantly grateful?

Traveling Light
Boughton, England

He has told you, O mortal, what is good; and what does the LORD require of you but to do justice, and to love kindness, and to walk humbly with your God?

MICAH 6:8

Please, oh, please, let this letter find its way into the hands of a friend I have never met. Someone who needs to feel the joy of letting go of old baggage and traveling lighter through this short and beautiful journey we have been offered. An old adage says that if you want to travel fast, travel alone, but if you want to travel far, travel in a community. But even beyond that, if you want to travel with depth, learn the names of the flowers along the way, fall in love a thousand times, believe that you can meet the demands of the suffering along the way, speak your truth to power, and live into the mission of your life. We need to travel together. It is community that truly allows us to travel light. This letter is written as a call for individuals to remember the need for community and to travel with others to see the fruition of dreams and the work of justice.

There are reasons to fear traveling light. We may fear that in traveling light there will not be enough—maybe there is only bread for 4,999. We can fear traveling with others and worry about what they think of us. Am I too Christian, or perhaps not Christian enough? What are they judging me on? My age? My weight? My politics? What if someone uncovers a shameful secret or my resentments or even my broken relationships? All of those fears we carry around like huge packages prevent us from being able to travel well together.

When we lay aside our fears, we travel more lightly. We discover there is enough for us when we travel together, that people want to hope with us, and that we can laugh easier and more often when we are together on the journey.

In our work at Thistle Farms it is critical for us to travel together. We have miles to go together in a world where more than a million people are trafficked, countless more addicted and trapped by institutional poverty and systemic injustice. What I have witnessed from women who have come seeking shelter is that they come with nothing, yet are so heavy. They are burdened by trauma and addiction, but also by shame and injustice. Weighed down by the experiences of childhood trauma and systems that not only allow them to fall through the cracks, but also open up chasms that seem inescapable.

On average, women who come to live in the Thistle Farms communities are first raped between the ages of seven and eleven and hit the streets in their teenage years. The trauma and scars of sexual violence are universal; individual women bear them on their bodies and in their spirits. "Rape the women, kill the village" is a dark and present reality today. As we have traveled around the globe making new partnerships with small women's social enterprises, we have heard the same stories told in different languages with heartbreaking nuances. Yet, these communities and enterprises, recommitted to helping women and leaving none behind, can see the village live again, with new light. It is not a dream or an idealized theology; traveling together is a practical way for us all to live.

Every one of us in justice work is asked to do more with less, take people's throwaways and make something spectacular from them so that more people will be inspired to donate. It is only when all of us in justice work join together, not separating issues and worrying about our small piece of the pie, that we create the lavish tapestry of love from our meager swatches of cloth. We need to travel together because we won't make it traveling alone in this work. In community, we can be both extravagant and economic, as resources are pooled, social media are utilized, and lavishness is poured out on us all. We can be extravagant and light! We can be a light movement that bears the burden of another. We can remember that a church without beggars is just a museum—maybe unburdened, but lost to its mission.

So let us keep traveling together, learning all the flowers along the way, healing as we go. Because it is the destination, not the journey, in some ways. Our destination is that all our journeys begin and end with God. Like Shana, Doris, Shelia, and Regina, we have everything we need already to make that trip, and we find ourselves . . . traveling light.

QUESTIONS FOR REFLECTION

1. Whose presence has lightened your travels in the past?
2. What journey are you perhaps still fearful of taking?

After the Blossom

From the Deep Woods in Southern Georgia

∿ The glory of youths is their strength, but the beauty of the aged is their gray hair.

PROVERBS 20:29

After the flowering of spring and the newness of being outside during the summer, there is a long pause. The dog days of summer, as corn hair has turned mahogany and Joe-Pye weed has grown taller than a man, are some of the longest for those seeking justice and raising money. In the Christian calendar, it is the long season after Pentecost that drags so long that for the faithful few who show up in August there is room to stretch out in the pews to hear old stories and believe they still hold new dreams. This is the letter to all of us living in that long dry season of life, when the kids are stretching out, when we have done the same work for decades, and when we see our hair begin to turn. August and the beginning of September of our years and lives are when the temperatures continue to reach sweltering heights, binding shirts to bodies in a sweaty grasp. Gangly twigs on tree limbs hang like moss on live oaks and leaves fall faint in the lazy summer afternoon.

The dog days can be a dangerous season for farming. It's too easy to lose track of the importance of this time for the harvest, serving to "make it or break it" for a bumper crop. It's the season of swarming bees and fully mature mosquitoes and ticks. The dry woods can flare up, and worry about health can begin to stir hearts at night. But this is also the quiet season when you can almost hear the moon rise and the roots stretching out for more water. The thistles have long abandoned their purple glory for a downy white. The mating has finished and fawns are walking a little distance from their does. It is all happening so quietly, in hushed stillness, that I have to be reminded I am spinning fast through a timeless universe.

We are all spinning through the dog days, even when we feel as if we are not even moving. That is the way of life, a complete stillness as time itself rushes toward something we cannot grasp. I marvel when I watch the sun on late afternoons. It doesn't move a degree in its huge arc as I sweat and walk. Time itself blurs as I try to imagine the roots growing new fingers in the thick dark earth beneath my steps. The woods are a patient teacher in her silent lesson of how, even in the heavy stillness of an afternoon, everything will pass by. This is the day for gray heads to dream new dreams, to celebrate the agelessness, not just the freshness of farming. Let us hold on to this day, the light, the shape of clouds, the size of our children's feet, because before our very eyes it will all pass us by . . . in the glory of a fall day that will proceed to the barrenness of winter and then on to a new life we may not even recognize.

QUESTIONS FOR REFLECTION

1. In your long, dry season, what new dreams may yet be yours to dream?

2. Do you feel yourself caught up in timeless spinning or in the motionlessness of a late autumn afternoon?

Pray without Ceasing

Preparing to Preach in Chattanooga, Tennessee

⁌ Rejoice always, pray without ceasing, give thanks in all cir-
cumstances; for this is the will of God in Christ Jesus for you

1 THESSALONIANS 5:16–18, ESV

When exhaustion or disaster hits the farm, we pray. We pray
for the rains to come as we do a dance. We pray for the rains to
stop and then we dig a ditch. Fear and weariness can bring the
strongest person to their knees in prayer. It doesn't have to be
a formal or rational prayer; "Please, God" is plenty. I think this
happens because there is still mystery in the tornado's path or
the shift of plate tectonics, shaking the earth. We don't know
when a baby will be born, and we wait for days for labor to
kick in. We sit vigil for days to be there for the uncertain moment when a loved one will take their last breath. There is still
mystery in this world that beckons us to stop and to keep vigil.
When we sit in vigil, the Spirit hovers close.

We may sit in wonder or dread but still we sit. In that sitting,
there is faith. In that sitting, there is love. And while we may
never know what effect our vigil had, we know we are changed
in the space. Our hearts may be empty, the flowing streams of
hope dried up, but we are still able to sit and so we offer that.
The pain of losing a crop, a home, a loved one can leave us feeling that we were tested in our faith and found wanting. Sometimes it seems the vanity and randomness of the world never
wearies and I wonder if that sense of despair will finally keep
me from sitting anymore. But in my life, on my farm, I have

learned that trials and disasters are not a test; the spring will always come. It is not a test of my faith when bad things come, but it is my faith that carries me through the bad days.

Something buried deep within me does not stop praying. Some seed of hope blooms despite the darkness I cast around it. I kiss a friend good-bye, I stack bricks that have been scattered by category 5 tornadoes, I go to a prison and sit with someone who has been given a life sentence and the sun rises on the 100 millionth day of creation. Then I dust myself off and turn over the earth again with a simple prayer for peace.

QUESTIONS FOR REFLECTION

1. What event outside of your control causes you concern?

2. What practice of stillness might allow you to see that concern differently?

You Can Forget How to Farm, or Ride a Bike

Nashville, Tennessee

∾ For where two or three are gathered in my name, I am there among them.

MATTHEW 18:20

I took my bike into the bike shop over a year ago. It was a used racing bike with a red seat, super thin tires, and a fancy gearing system. My life got busy and, like baking bread and knitting, biking became a hobby that took a back burner to pastoring a church, mothering children, growing a social enterprise, and trying to stave off the encroaching e-mails that fill my inbox and my mind. Then last week I got my bike out of the shop. Amid the noise and haste of my world, it was time to reclaim the solitary life of a cyclist who rides the back roads alone and thinks lofty thoughts with the wind rushing by. I went straight from the shop to the Greenways, with its more than twelve miles of hilly circuitous route, and started riding uphill. I clicked the front gear down as low as it could go and clicked the back gear, which was on the highest position. I needed to click the back gears into the lowest position to ascend this first hill after a year of cyclist dormancy. I couldn't find a gear click on the handlebars to make it work. I tried everything. I turned around and went downhill, fumbled with pushing the gears at the same time, pushing the two gears I could find in the opposite directions and clicking twice. Nothing. I was stuck in midgear and couldn't get up the hill. Oh my lord, I thought, I have forgotten how to ride this bike. I thought you couldn't forget. Of course I also once believed that M&Ms didn't melt in your hands and that if I could get "caught up," life after that would be smooth sailing.

So after one more failed attempt, in complete humiliation, I got off my bike and started walking toward the car. On the way back, a man with a similar gearing system was coming up the hill at a pretty fast clip. "Excuse me," I lied, "I am borrowing this bike and I don't know how to change gears. Can you help me?" Halfway up that steep hill he stopped. He got off his bike and showed me how to push the brakes sideways so they could act as gears and shift the back gear lower. "Thank you so much," I said as I watched the sweat pour from his gallant face. Then he picked up my bike and with one hand changed the gears and with the other moved the pedals so that the bike would be in the lowest gear for my next shot at climbing the hill. "It's actually my bike and I am so pathetic I have forgotten how to use it," I blabbed, as if he is my confessor. "No problem" this modern-day Buddha responds as soon as he sees I now can climb the hill. I feel like weeping. Sometimes I hate how much I still need people. Dare I say "strangers."

This Good Samaritan reminded me that a spiritual journey is not a competition. It is a journey that we take alone, yet with one another as friends and companions. Church is not a competition. There will always be greater and lesser churches, there will always be more well-funded groups and not-for-profits who are struggling more than you. This journey is about coming together and helping one another make it to the shore.

Jesus reminds us that whenever two or more are gathered together in his name, he is with us. When people join together in love and partnership, our Lord is right there. I felt it easily on the trail with the man who stopped and taught me once again how to ride without a single word of ridicule. We can remind one another what it is to farm, to pray, and to bike.

The spiritual journey is not a competition. It is a joining together of us all, so that when two or three are gathered, the

Spirit rests among us. We are to share all on this journey: our knowledge, our burdens, and our visions. We are called to share everything. If we have five loaves and two fishes, we share it all with five thousand. If we have two cloaks, we are asked to give one to anyone who asks.

If two or three are gathered in the name of justice, it is tender and assuring. If two or three hundred are gathered, it is inspiring. Now we are gathering two or three thousand and are watching as they are inspired to make a difference in their communities and the world. I am thinking now about the miracle of two or three hundred thousand, slowly joining one another in a movement for healing and hope for survivors around the globe. This miracle means we continue to teach without ridicule, share what we have, and recognize the Spirit in our midst.

QUESTIONS FOR REFLECTION

1. What belief of yours has changed over time?
2. What unexpected act of kindness has reminded you about the best in people?

Searching for the Heart of Farming
Charlottesville, Virginia

⌒ Let the sea roar, and all that fills it; the world and those who live in it. Let the floods clap their hands; let the hills sing together for joy at the presence of the LORD.

PSALM 98:7–9

The rolling hills of Virginia in the fall look like a painter's hand found the translucent colors and splashed the canvas. It's a festival of wonder: the canopy of trees turning old woods into stained-glass cathedrals. It is easy to worship in this hallowed space and to feel the connection between the heavens and the earth. The bright yellow walnut leaves set the valleys aglow against their stark black bark. The vibrant oranges of maple trees fill any pilgrim with the hope of transformation. The stunning burnt red of the dogwoods calls our hearts to remember the tender spring and the fullness of time. Connecting nature to the holy is the one of the great gifts that farmers cultivate. People connect to the eternal through music, meditation, and especially the earth. It's all about the idea that we have been searching for our hearts forever, yet every now and then in the glory of fall or in the beauty of sound we find it and remember that we hold an eternal love within our temporal bodies. Farmers seeing their pumpkins come into their ripeness, pastors seeing their congregations gathered by riversides in spring, and fishermen seeing a brown trout jump all share the same glory of feeling a fleeting reunion with that most sacred truth: We are already in eternity, living with God. This is heaven on earth. This is the beginning of the forever. We are in the midst of the writing of a psalm of praise to our creator.

Celebrating the beauty of the earth is a grace that washes over all of us as we love with abandonment for a moment, maybe for a lifetime. It is a glimpse that peeks around the bend in the river as we marvel at the magnificence of fall under harvest moons and brightly hued trees. Sometimes it's just a moment of unbounded joy so powerful it sets us free. Please let this letter remind you to open your eyes and your hands and your ears to take in the glory unfolding around us. Let it connect your heart to the truth that we are living in eternity now.

QUESTIONS FOR REFLECTION

1. Where do you experience a larger, mysterious presence?
2. What new place of reverence might be waiting?

Trolling Is Not Farming

*Walking through the Vanderbilt Campus,
Nashville, Tennessee*

∿ What? know ye not that your body is the temple of the
Holy Ghost which is in you, which ye have of God, and ye are not
your own?

1 CORINTHIANS 6:19 (KJV)

Let this letter be a sweet reminder to us all in the work of planting hope and faith: we have to think about what our actions
mean for others. We are always called to remember as farmers
that everything we do has consequences; that we never know
whom we are hurting or who is listening to us as we go about
our days. Farmers and all workers in the vineyard need to remember the mantra, "do no harm."

I was walking through the campus where I have been a pastor for twenty years and could almost write the dialogue for
the scene I saw playing out before me. It was the first day of
classes in the new semester. A young graduate student was
walking beside her professor who looked to be her senior
by about forty years. I could imagine he had taken all the re-
quired sexual misconduct classes. I could imagine she saw
herself as a young, independent woman who didn't fall for the
drunken fraternity mess where most of the sexual violence on
campus is centered. I could imagine him twenty years earlier,
not finding love in his native country. I walked behind them,
but my fifty-year-old self was invisibly present to the charged
air that surrounded them. "Yes, yes," she exclaimed, talking
about his philosophical lecture. She said that the class was an
"aha" moment that had opened her in a way she never knew

was possible. He was gazing at her and I could hardly make out the beautifully accented hushed tones of what he was saying. They walked together in perfect sync. "I can't believe that we have such a similar view of the world," she said, launching into a long talk complete with huge gestures that bump her arms against his. I want to stop them and say to him, "Don't." Don't do this, even though it's sexy and feeds your ego. I want to say to her, "Don't." Don't do this, even though you are mesmerized by his thoughts and his position of power on this campus. Somehow without meaning to, I have turned an afternoon walk into an undercover stalking event. They continued to walk so closely together that it became impossible to hear them, and then they turned to walk down a smaller path less hurried and occupied.

I remember similar conversations from decades ago. The events between the grad student and professor are what we in the business call a "trigger" for me. Triggers are the events that bring up old memories and set you off down a road of anxiety and fear. What this event triggered in me is the heartbreaking truth that we give ourselves away for almost nothing for fear of being alone or unimportant. It kills me that in spite of any training or knowledge we have, we still can be mesmerized by the thought of possessing another. There is a lingering brokenness and misuse of sexuality that prevents us from living fully into our gifts and from appreciating the gifts of others. I don't know why it was so plain and powerful to me on this walk, but it was.

Perhaps it seemed so obvious because he was not skilled at playing the role of a dedicated farmer/teacher using his gifts to plant new knowledge in the mind of his students. I could see in his words and body language that he was ready to pounce and make a catch of this young and eager prey. Perhaps the scene felt obvious because I remember the conversation with a math professor years ago as I debated in my head just how far I might go to secure a friendship that he wanted, one that would benefit me in the system. When I think of the farm and how to nurture and love it, we need to remember the difference between good farmers that plant good seeds and predatory trollers. We need to work toward creating safe sanctuaries, believing young women and men who have been sexually assaulted and holding more powerful people accountable for taking advantage.

QUESTIONS FOR REFLECTION

1. In what ways have you misused, or been tempted to misuse, your relationship with someone?

2. "We give ourselves away for almost nothing for fear of being alone. . . ." True?

Imagining the Harvest
Charlotte, North Carolina

Do you not say, "Four months more, then comes the harvest"? But I tell you, look around you, and see how the fields are ripe for harvesting.

JOHN 4:35

I was walking along a river in the glory of North Carolina's hills, talking to a fellow priest. The stunning autumn landscape and waterfalls were the perfect backdrop for the question he asked—"What insight could you share with me that might help to inspire my congregation?" What a beautiful question to ask someone you trust enough to say what is truly in your heart. The answer would not be a list of "four things every pastor should know to grow a congregation" gleaned from a professional seminar.

As soon as the question was asked, I began imagining where the water from that ever-flowing stream meandering beside us was going. I could see it begin to move more quickly and imagined that it was heading rapidly toward the shore from the steep granite mountains from which it was cascading. I had just read a slave narrative in which the slave imagined freedom long before his shackles were broken and removed. And I remembered the previous week in California, when I received the means to form the global alliance of women's cooperatives with funding for a year. That funding came from the imaginings of a group of friends a few years before, dreaming about how we could offer a shared trade option for women producers. So I looked at my dear friend and said, "Imagine it."

I am profoundly humbled and in awe of the imagination we hold. Daydreaming is the cheapest and best gift of a rich interior life.

Farmers need to imagine a rich harvest. To see in their minds the sweet shade of green of that misty morning when the harvest begins even as they plant. They can, if they give themselves space, conjure up the exact hue of purple before the lavender is reaped. For everyone working hard in the field: give yourself the gift of imagining so deeply that you can describe the shimmer of the golden hair hay that dances with sunlight and wind after all the work is done. Such a lavish imagination will reflect the stunning beauty of God's creation and joy.

Living in the moment can include dreaming of a blessed tomorrow. Years of imagining can enrich memory as well as vision. I believe someday I will be able to sit with memory and recall the rich imagination of my life. Memory can become a great source of company, deepening as it increases over the years. I can already feel that I have a foretaste of the sweetness and refined nature of memory as we age. Sometimes I imagine those future memories becoming a valued old brandy sitting on the shelf of my interior life, burning the back of my throat as I take a swig. Imagination and memory allow me to travel easily in time and space with dreams free to take root or flight. Imagination and memory carry us to sacred ground where we can plant ourselves in the holy ground of hope.

QUESTIONS FOR REFLECTION

1. What dreams and visions is God providing through your memories and imagination?

2. What vision, perhaps unspoken until now, is ready to be shared with another?

Winter

Signs of Life
From a Deathbed in Tennessee

⟋⟍ The kingdom of heaven is like a merchant in search of fine pearls; on finding one pearl of great value, he went and sold all that he had and bought it.

MATTHEW 13:45–46

There is radiance to a faithful farmer who is in contemplation of death. The rich soil of silence, prayer, and action blossoms a hundredfold as such a farmer reaps a harvest even as they grieve. It's like a field of sunflowers in late August lifting their heads toward the sun in rows sown by patience and compassion.

I entered a friend's house to say good-bye and found myself sitting by the recliner at her feet, letting tears flow as she spoke, her head propped up by two pillows. While we talked, her husband, who is an amazing Episcopal priest, blessed us and the children and grandchildren with communion as he played a song about a simple life. Her daughter wiped her mouth with a sponge, joining me on the floor on the other side of her chair. The grandkids played with toys close by as her sister made sure that visitors were quiet and the kitchen was ready in case anyone could muster hunger between the waves of grief washing over the whole beloved family.

This wise woman filled with the inner light of love told me about three things she had learned from me, what she was grateful for, and then said that life is really about learning to say hello and good-bye. She gave me a scarf and a pair of earrings she loved and I knew that this is what grace looks like in flesh and bone. Grace is tender and generous, not boastful or weighed down by the baggage of what might have been. It is quiet and manages a compassionate smile even as others weep. It is as beautiful as that late summer field of sunflowers. It is a moment that we cannot hold onto.

It is so hard to witness the dying of a friend, especially one who has been a means of so much grace for so many people. Grace is more than mercy; it offers us comfort when we didn't even think we should ask. In grace there is no shame, only radiant love that so fills the space that we remember we are all one. At her feet I could feel the grief of kissing my mother good-bye twenty years ago, of a friend who had passed a few months earlier, of my sister's death last year, of all the tears cried in all the fields where people have buried the bones and ashes of those they hold dearest in this world, unable to imagine flowers blooming again in the fields where we learned we are dust. As I leaned in, I asked her for a blessing. She offered me the blessing she said her mother gave her. As we hugged and I felt the bones of her frail body, I knew that in my lifetime I would rarely be in the presence of a farmer who grew anything more beautiful or feel the strong sinews of one formed so completely of something holy as well as earthly. I whispered to her, "I hope you dive into it when the moment comes." "Me too," she said. "Say a good word for us." "I'll try."

I can't remember what else was said. I remember her husband walking me out and thinking how their love for one another was a seal upon their hearts and a crown upon their foreheads and that all the two of them do is manifest love around them because they are so full. That would be the last time I saw her, and as I pulled away I prayed she had a sense for the magnificent field of flowers, children, love, and compassion she has sown in the hearts and minds of so many. She is beautiful.

QUESTIONS FOR REFLECTION

1. What unexpected, simple gifts of grace have been given to you?

2. Where might God be calling you to give such a gift to another?

Stand in the Field of Hope
Northern Rwanda

⟋‾‾ Then justice will dwell in the wilderness, and righteousness abide in the fruitful field.

ISAIAH 32:16

With barely the memory of old clothes, children of poor farmers carry yellow plastic water containers uphill on red dirt
roads beside rich fields of maize, bananas, and cassava. The
task looks as endless as the memories of genocide that twenty
years later still forms the context for everything unfolding on
our drive toward the geranium field that supplies the oils we
use at Thistle Farms in Nashville. The roads that carried us to
this field were built by some of the perpetrators of the genocide and partially paid for by a world that turned its back on
the million or more people who died in less than three months
after decades of hatred propagated by a culpable government.
Scattered in these fields today are women farmers. This letter
is written in their honor, true heroes of the truth that hope cannot be killed. You can break it, you can beat the living hell out
of it, you can strip it of all reasonable doubt, but the seeds of
hope will not be killed. If we simply nurture these seeds, they
can yield a thousandfold.

The women farming these fields are the survivors of genocide. Genocide. Genocide. It is hard to fathom the rape, death,
and mutilation they not only survived but have relived in trau-
matic memory for more than twenty years. They have endured
the yoke of learning to forgive neighbors and grieving their
children simultaneously. In 2001, these "preachers of hope,"
these living examples of the beatitude that those who mourn

will be blessed, began a cooperative to grow geranium. From the profits they are able to build houses and support one another as they heal from their trauma. Behind each introduction made by the director of the program, Nicolas Hitimana, are the whispered stories of these women who lost so much in 1994. As we shake hands and greet each other, I try to mouth the only word I know in Kinyarwanda, "Muraho." I feel another wave of tears press behind my eyes as I try to take in the bright sunlight, the fields, and the stories. Genocide is not like a tsunami; its devastating waves crash for decades as people continue to farm in the same fields where they buried their dead and now make the heroic effort to proclaim that healing is possible.

And so, in the daily task of watering and weeding, buying new fields and planting new hope, these women, with turbans of brightly colored fabrics wound around their heads, preach that the most sacred ground we walk on is forgiveness. It is not forgetting, it is not dismissing these crimes; it is the simple truth that when we forgive, we are able to find freedom, to live and to allow the hope still dormant in our hearts to blossom. I am in love with the women, the fragrance of geranium, and its ability to bring new life in the driest season. Standing in a field of hope is a holy shrine where the Spirit is thick. Please, God, let us learn the lesson of forgiveness and hope's intertwining.

QUESTIONS FOR REFLECTION

1. Where is forgiveness needed in your life?
2. If you can see that place as a dry field, what first step can you take to help "carry water" there?

Go to the Prison
to Seek Jesus

From the Women's Prison
in Nashville, Tennessee

⟋⟍ Let the oppressed see it and be glad; you who seek God, let your hearts revive. For the LORD hears the needy, and does not despise his own that are in bonds.

PSALM 69:32–33

I have heard volunteers in prison chaplaincy programs say that they "carry Jesus into prisons." I am writing this letter to pastors and preachers and volunteers, urging them to take another sip of humility and to remember that if Jesus's spirit is alive anywhere in this world, he is alive and living with prisoners. A few years ago, a young deacon with whom I worked struggled to write sermons. She could spend twenty hours or so tucked away in a library with volumes of theology to decode some beautiful and yet hollow meanings from the Gospel stories. I remember her admirable and earnest love of preaching and wishing for her that when she struggled to write a sermon, she would visit a prison for the afternoon, not the library. From behind the locked prison gates the gospel sounds different. When you preach to women wearing matching blue outfits with nothing to their name except what people put on their commissary cards, the message gets clearer. When I go to prison, sometimes it feels as if the Gospel stories are living in the faces I see and echoing off the "wailing walls" where people long to feel freedom. In prison, whether as a visitor or an inmate, you remember your humanity and the need for people to be merciful.

There is so much injustice in our prison systems. While America has the highest per capita prison rate with over 2 million inmates, we still live under the illusion that justice is served in our system. A national study by a New Mexico task force showed that over 85 percent of incarcerated women are survivors of severe childhood trauma, including sexual assault. On average, the women served in Magdalene are first assaulted between the ages of seven and eleven. The abuse perpetrated on our children becomes a red carpet to the gated community of ongoing trauma and depression called prison.

The spirit of love is especially thick in the midst of injustice. And when we remember all the internal, as well as external, prisons of our lives, we can begin to feel the gift of the spirit enter our hearts as well. We want to serve others in response to the gospel. And when we serve others, we feel the Gospel stories come alive for us. So when you can't preach, go to prison, and let it preach to you.

QUESTIONS FOR REFLECTION

1. To what foreign/dark/uncomfortable place have you been beckoned?
2. Are you there to speak, or to listen?

Our Last Remains

On a Path near Oxford, England

For I am convinced that neither death, nor life, nor angels, nor rulers, nor things present, nor things to come, nor powers, nor height, nor depth, nor anything else in all creation, will be able to separate us from the love of God in Christ Jesus our Lord.

ROMANS 8:38–39

Walking along the Thames around noon, I decided to tie my hair back. Digging deep into my pack, I found an old cloth ponytail holder a friend had given me on a hike a long time ago when I was in dire need of one. When she gave it to me, she told me it was the best kind, designed not to pull your hair. Now, after a hiking accident took her life and months after we laid her ashes to rest, I felt as if I was again holding her last remains. This small band of cloth that she casually handed me on a hike could be the last thing she touched that I will hold. We think of last remains as the body or the ashes, but there are a million smaller pieces that linger long after those we loved have passed away to tell the story of how they lived. I think about all the small things offered to friends and coworkers that might someday be my last remains for them. It makes all our small "little somethings" we give one another seem bigger. When give each other the shirts off our backs, the ponytail holders out of our hair, or a cup of cold water, those could be the small and beautiful things for which we are remembered. There are a million little "funerals" for those we love. When we actually lay each other down, in those small quiet remembrances, we grieve the unfathomable truth that we are temporal bodies, holding eternal love.

I remember sitting in my house a year after my mother's death and finding a strand of her long brown hair that must have escaped her ever-present braid. I took the hair and walked it into the woods, wondering how long it would take to lay all of her to rest. So far it has taken twenty years. I still find pieces of her in the scarring on the dining room table I inherited, the smile on my youngest son's face, and in the practical nature of farming that I embrace. My mother liked things to be useful and I can still feel her spirit echoing in my voice as I remind people to treat the work more like farming. My mom grew up on a dairy farm, and whether it was snowing or hot, Christmas or New Year's, the cows were milked and the crops gathered into barns. She would be tender, but only to a point. She would allow sickness in us, but only for so long. Then she would say, get up and get going. I can hear her as I talk with women in recovery trying to overcome more trauma than I can imagine. It also brings her close as I walk that fine line between tenderness and firmness. You are carrying the last remains of those you loved and who loved you. It may be a story, or some little trinket, it could be an heirloom or burden. But we carry those we love pretty close. The finest gift is when an unexpected remain of theirs comes to us and we are washed in their love all over again.

The simple green cloth I held in my hand on that day felt like a holy relic. It was just like her to give a little something out of the blue. How easy to imagine her last remains like socks, ponytail holders, and wonderful stories and memories scattered all across the country amongst her friends.

QUESTIONS FOR REFLECTION

1. What unexpected gifts of remembrance can you recall?

2. How have these gifts informed your belief about your own life? Your ministry?

Preach Love,
Truth Will Follow

Ecuador

⌁ If it is possible, so far as it depends on you, live peaceably with all.

ROMANS 12:18

Farming on hillsides is dizzying to watch. In the rich volcanic soil near the Black Sheep Inn in Ecuador, the slope of the landscape is dramatic. Rounding the steep bends to the top can generate vertigo, traveling from sea level to thirteen thousand feet in a few hours. I layered on more clothes as the air thinned, trying to match the falling temperature as the clouds hovered nearby. There was a point on this journey where I thought our bus was not going to make it. I joked with my fellow travelers that this was it and offered a "last rites" sort of blessing as we careened around another hairpin turn on a road not quite wide enough for two vehicles, especially if one of them was a bus. The whole time we were climbing, traditionally dressed farmers scurried up the mountain with bags of corn on their backs or worked fields at what appeared to be about a thirty-degree slope. The fields looked like quilts crisscrossing over mountains with a batting of clouds as these farmers, with precision and patience, stitched lines of corn and grains. It's hard to imagine the strength needed to cultivate and carry crops to town in northern Ecuador. Farmer's hearts and lungs must be huge, with no need to count calories or worry about getting thirty minutes of vigorous exercise.

Watching them till the soil and weed among the corn would clear up any romantic notion of farming. It is a gander at the hard truth of it. Seeing the women, with single braids and layers of clothing around their bodies and their bowed legs, I had a glimpse into the certainty that true farming takes perseverance and a surrender to the land you have been given. This is the land they were born into and this is the land they know. It is the land upon which they grow the food to feed their families and so this is the land they love—for better or worse, richer or poorer, in sickness and in health, until death where they are reunited. That is the truth of farming and that is the truth of our lives. We don't need to sugarcoat it; it is a stunning story and a vision of the kingdom. When we really see this world, and see ourselves in it, we remember that the best we can do is preach love and see how truth follows. I do not know the truth of the lives of any of the people I watch through my window. I am not called to change any of it. You and I are called to love the world, the world that is before us. Sometimes, in order to love it well, we need to be willing to change. Our truth and understanding will evolve and deepen as we preach love in our daily lives through our actions. It is a daunting task to try to love the whole world one person at a time, but that is the task of being a disciple.

QUESTIONS FOR REFLECTION

1. What (or who) is the hillside to be farmed in your life?

2. In what ways might that hillside be a gift, rather than a burden to you?

Nurture the Silence
Where Transcendence
Is Cultivated
Manitucky Island in Canada

⌒ For he is our God, and we are the people of his pasture,
and the sheep of his hand. O that today you would listen to his voice!
PSALM 95:7

This letter is a prayer for silence. It's possible to be in a space
without noise and still not cultivate a space for silence. In those
times we are just preoccupied by the voices in our heads and
all the worries on our hearts. There can be as much noise inside as outside of us in this world. Making a space for silence
means we let the murkiness of the whirling eddies of anxiety
and anticipation settle and become still. Then the water clears
and we can see all the way to the bottom of the deep pool that
dwells in us.

Silence is perhaps the most neglected and most needed
resource for growing rich in faith. Silence is the way to communion. There is no prayer without some silence and there is
nowhere to grow silence like a quiet day alone among pine
trees and rocks. The smell of pine needles blended with the
profound stillness of rocks offers a feast of contemplation for
people whose spirits are famished from the endless noise and
haste of this world. Soft moss and tatted lichen are the fair linens on rocks transformed into unpolished altars. Birdsong is
the call to worship with no need for words. When it is quiet
enough, I swear you can hear the memory of any rock. Rock

absorbs heat, water, wind, and time like no other element. It can take your stress and hold your story. It provides a safe place to be completely silent, letting the earth spin by itself. Rock is in no hurry to change or move and, sitting on this altar in sunshine, the rock's heat absorbs into your body with a quiet that was mastered more than a million years before you were born. On such rocks, among scattered birch trees emerging from silty soil, I felt a silence grow so rich that words would have been an intrusion. This silence is thick and has a tender fragrance. Something deeper is speaking to the sacred space that lives between our head and heart . . . where the soul dwells and invites the listener to a reverent peace. In this patch of farm we are in the presence of a universal invitation to a sacred place—one that exists beside still waters, where we are comforted by the truth that all is love. There is no need to write letters or speak of this internal sacred space except to say that such Good News needs to be shared among farmers who want to cultivate peace. We can remind each other, amid the noise and haste, that there is peace. And we can find our way into this peaceful silence in the rocks scattered among the fields and farms. We can find silence in them and share a sweet communion.

QUESTIONS FOR REFLECTION

1. Where does your yearning for peace take you?
2. Can you cultivate the soil of silence to bear more fruit in you?

Fast from Everything
You Love Once in a While
Phoenix, Arizona

⁓ And the Spirit immediately drove him out into the wilderness. He was in the wilderness for forty days, tempted by Satan; and he was with the wild beasts; and the angels waited on him.

MARK 1:12–13

May this letter be a gentle reminder about the disciplined faith of farmers! I love the landscape of Phoenix, where the desert and heat call us to cultivate a beautiful starkness in our own hearts. On this land I am grateful for the Desert Fathers and Mothers who lived and taught fasting and prayer so powerfully that we look to them as guides more than a thousand years later.

The Desert Fathers teach us what an exceptional virtue it is to foster our spiritual lives by periodic fasting, as it strengthens our souls and offers a way to cleanse our hearts and minds. Fasting, they believed, can whither up thoughts of anger or bitterness and offer enlightenment. Farming offers a certain pace to life missed by those of us unaccustomed to seasons of growing, including time to let a field lie fallow. There is an illusion within the busyness of life that if we work fast enough and hard enough without stopping, we will accomplish more and more. But the truth is, we just end up starving. When we spend our days always trying to gather, the crops die and we burn out. Feasting without a fast every now and then is just gluttony. There is no reason to suffer burnout if we allow an ebb and flow to our days, to our feasting, and to our fields.

What I am talking about is not just taking a break, but being disciplined enough to fast from everything we love once in a while. Whether that is work, food, or phones, such an ebb and flow leaves us feeling more balanced and better able to serve our communities, feeling energized and humble. There is nothing like a good fast to humble the spirit. As humans we can get hooked by our need to fill ourselves, a desire to numb our senses, a hunger to have and experience everything. There is nothing finer (or saner) than to experience a productive fast and then celebrate with a feast. Some of the best fasts are offered with intention. It could be a fast with the intention of gaining clarity, offered for the sake of another person, in protest with others, or for penitential purposes. World religions all offer days for communities to come together and fast, to remember who we are and whose we are. Those are considered some of the holiest days of the year.

Once about 150 pastors in Tennessee came together for a three-day fast. Our purpose was to protest the health-care cuts destined to hit the most vulnerable folks in our state. I remember feeling so close to rabbis, imams, and ministers. Throughout the protest we wrote to each other and gathered together at the end of the three days at a Jewish temple. It was a rich time and even as I write this letter I want to fast again. I don't want to live in gluttony. I want to turn off my phone, cancel all my meetings, and spend a rich and glorious day fasting and remembering myself as a child of God.

QUESTIONS FOR REFLECTION

1. To help you focus attention, from what can you fast?
2. As you reflect on this season of your life, what new daily prayer might you offer?

The Loneliness
of Community
San Eduardo, Ecuador

⟨⟩ Then the Lord God said, "It is not good that the man should be alone; I will make him a helper as his partner."

GENESIS 2:18

There is a farming community about three and half hours north of Guayaquil, Ecuador, that I have visited annually for more than eighteen years, for about nine days at a time. It is here that I have been the loneliest. It has been a great gift to return every year to this same field with cacao and bananas in the midst of a huge community and remember that there is a tender, solitary loneliness in the midst of community. Maybe this letter will find its way into the hands of one who feels the internal struggle or who wonders if anyone else knows how lonely it is sometimes.

Throughout the year we are in touch weekly with this Ecuadorian community regarding the school, clinic, and social enterprise we helped to open and continue to fund. Then once a year a group of doctors, students, musicians, and entrepreneurs pack their gear and their lofty ideas and head down for a visit. It's quite a big reunion, getting off the rented bus, lugging our nets and bags that will be laid out on the concrete church floor. We have a big fiesta and the kids play music and people dance and eat. It's then that I feel the gradual return of an unchosen gift. It calls me to set myself on the outside and watch it all. Later I will use what I see to gather folks around the light of a candle, offering a reflection on that . . . and each day's work.

Before dawn the next day I am alert and anticipating the day, the struggles within the group, the million questions, trying to remember the names of folks I haven't seen in a year, and wondering if those huge green caterpillars on the ground will bite me if I get up before light. Part of me loves the loneliness and the disconnect I feel during these times, and part of me longs for a week in which I don't wrestle with guilt, pity, anger, and fatigue in the midst of joy and gratitude.

If we take the work we do as vocation and use it for prayer and service, we are going to get lonely. I think it is part of the journey of the heart. The sometimes overwhelming sense of loneliness is just one of the gifts of leadership and I do not want to stay on it too long, or else it will become self-serving and pointless. Loneliness can be the by-product of truth seeking and soul searching. It is the wonder of being in community and having a pilgrim's heart.

QUESTIONS FOR REFLECTION

1. In your solitary times, what gifts have you received?

2. In your times of community, what gifts have you been able to give?

Farming Is Timeless, but We Are Given Only a Number of Seasons

～ For everything there is a season, and a time for every matter under heaven.

ECCLESIASTES 3:1

The bluebells never age. Every spring we greet them a year older and they, in their sweet perennial joy, remain forever young. I have seen the same bluebells blooming in fields I have walked for thirty years. I have walked those trails newly in love, grieving death, pushing the stroller for my newborns, and praying for those same children as they bound forward in their own lives. I have dreamed new dreams in the splendor of their tender pinks and blues, signs of spring that expand our hearts in fresh soil. I have pledged to keep walking with a spirit of renewal, observing their passing beauty as a sign of the tender way that time slips by our guarded hearts. I love the bluebells and maybe a tiny part of me envies their timeless way of living. Bluebells live in the yellow mornings, watching the sun as it stretches out longer in the sky.

Now when I walk past the bluebells, I can feel the tendernss of the eternal passing of seasons and times. Now I walk by the bluebells with no children in tow and hear new moms pushing strollers with friends and chatting about the number of hours their baby kept them up the night before. They have no idea that very soon that season will fade, maybe as quickly as the fading of the bluebell blossoms, and their children will walk on their own. They will remember, as in all fading dreams, the way it was when they were young, when dreams outnumbered memory. And for them another spring will come when they walk by the bluebells and wonder where the time went, how they got such a furrowed brow, and how the bluebells could possibly look younger and sweeter than they did just a season ago. I know that there will be a season in the not too distant future when I will share the soil with the bluebells and experience spring from the other side of time. On this side though, the springs come round and round and call us to celebrate the youthful gift that spring offers, reminding us to live in the present season and behold the beauty of the earth.

QUESTIONS FOR REFLECTION

1. In what ways do you guard your heart to the passage of time?

2. How might you honor with more intentionality your season of life?

Find the Lost Sheep
Somewhere on an Old Country Road, Tennessee

⟡ Which one of you, having a hundred sheep and losing one of them, does not leave the ninety-nine in the wilderness and go after the one that is lost until he finds it?

LUKE 15:4

Years ago I got lost and drove onto an old country road that looked forlorn and abandoned. It was a cold day and the land was full gray from the exposed limestone that made it poor country for farming. There were three old buzzards sitting in a barren hackberry tree on my left, and a cabin with a worn-out rebel flag hanging from the clothesline near a pile of trash and old tires. Across the road was a fenced-in field with just one sheep, looking abandoned and alone. It was the clearest image I have ever seen of the parable of the lost sheep in which Jesus tells us to leave the ninety-nine in search of the one forsaken.

It is the image that I carry with me when I meet folks who are broken, or just coming from the streets, or bearing the news of tragedy. It is the image of all of us, lost and wandering in a field of uncertainty. In that lost sheep I can see the faces of people so despairing they almost dared someone to offer them a sign of hope.

I abhor that place and the anger and fear it stirs up in me. I want to run from it and mourn the part in all of us that knows what it is to be the lost sheep. I want to fight the world that is harsh enough to make us feel we are standing between buzzards and useless old flags. But the parable of the lost sheep is a parable about compassion, humility, idealism, and, ultimately, love. Jesus is talking to the growing crowd that is following him to Jerusalem, where they will find themselves as lost as a lone sheep in winter. He is telling them that even in the hardest times, they are never abandoned. Into this place love goes with you. Jesus is reminding us that as followers of the way, those are the very places where we are called to go. We go remembering our own fears, and like love itself, we help each other find our way back. This gospel preaches that Love steps into the fearful places where we worry and despair . . . and finds us.

The lost sheep is the call to idealism: to live in hope with courage that no one is outside of love's embrace. When we encounter a woman on the streets so victimized she could not even identify where she lived on a map, we don't give up but find a way to welcome her home. Idealism says there is no one on all of God's green earth who is hopeless. The lost sheep is a call to humility. In humility we find the courage to face huge and unmovable systems—whether justice, education, or corrections—and work on behalf of those who have been marginalized. While mindful of our means and strength, we keep walking toward the gates with love, even toward the gates of the city that kills its prophets, never abandoning those who are oppressed.

The lost sheep is a call to community. Community is the very thing a sheep longs for more than anything else. It is through the gift of traveling together we lessen the chance we'll get lost. We make room for people to walk their individual path with friends who are heading in the same direction.

The gospel message of the lost sheep reminds us that farming is not a theory. It is more than a way of being: it is a call to action. Living faithfully has always been about the lost sheep, whether in standing up for gay and lesbian rights, or welcoming women from our streets and prisons with housing and jobs and family, or speaking up for a rape victim on campus. Luke's Gospel should embolden us to look again at the abandoned fields of this world and make a path wide enough for the sheep to come home.

I have learned so much from people who came to find me when I was lost, standing with my back against the wind, hoping someone would be idealistic and gracious enough to see me. I have been changed by the folks in this community who love heroically in their work and in their lives: people who travel to the margins of this city and to the ends of the earth to help the lost sheep. Going to find the lost sheep means calling on every city to provide long-term free housing for the survivors of trafficking, prostitution, addiction, and violence. For many folks here it means growing the work in faraway fields, pouring their hearts into the work of justice for others who seek freedom. For others here it means working hard right in their own backyard, for the equality in rites and rituals for every person. For all of us it means we stand together and work toward the well-being of others in the name of Love.

Sometimes I am the lost sheep. Sometimes you are the lost sheep. Together we find our way to Love, then go back and search the lonely ridges for those who are missing, to bring a message of unfathomable Love to others. When the sheep comes home, there is rejoicing—testimony to the truth that in the end Love is more powerful than anything that wants to wound us, abandon us, or make us feel alone.

QUESTIONS FOR REFLECTION

1. What gift have you received at a time when you were lost?

2. What unfamiliar road beckons you to go and to trust those who would travel with you?

Ending Full Circle,
at the Beginning

⟶ And so the farm goes to seed. When seed gets buried in the ground, it breaks down its hard outer shell and new sprouts emerge. It's not that different for us. We are dust and to dust we shall return. We are so much like the fields we tend. All our journeys begin and end with God; the sign of life is how we make our song, even at our grave. That is the truth of farming and the truth of our faith. We must lie down at the end of the journey and simply, somehow, go to seed. My mom used to say that when she died, she would be fine with being dirt or an angel. She felt that both were useful and important in carrying out the work of God. I have to believe that in the end we will become a bit of both. While we can't fully grasp it within our temporal minds, something more comes from an eternal love rooted within the spirits of our mostly dirt bodies. I want in the end to sing praises like the sun does every evening in bands of orange and pink. I want to remember how much I loved living and celebrate the gifts I have known like the dandelions that scatter confetti seeds on the wisp of winds. I want to dance like the waves in a perfect chorus line that is the culmination of the temporal and eternal meeting on the shore. When I go to seed, I want to bow my head like the trout lily in the graceful afternoon sunlight, warming hearts more than fields. In those holy moments when death meets with faith, there remains hope. We can take heart that the law of love, written in the fabric of creation, is firmly planted in the fields. There is nowhere that faith cannot grow. It can grow and thrive in us and, by God, beyond us. It can call us to humility and wholeness and we can dive into the return to the earth, just as we dove into our being at our birth.

> Love always has the last word. That truth gives me hope
> that in simplicity we can find our way to heaven.
> And, that in the end, truth
> will reassure us that we
> were enough.

—BECCA STEVENS

A Closing Litany for
Farmers of All Sorts of Fields
in the World

In the spirit of mercy, that is wide and solid as the ground upon which we make our stand, let us pray to our God.

Lord, have mercy

Holy One, we give you thanks for the gifts of mercy others have given us. We give you thanks for the brave farmers who have planted the seeds from which we reap. Help us remember the times when we were hungry, afraid, sick, or imprisoned by all the bonds that would keep us tied down. May that mercy be forged into compassion that loves the whole world without judgment. Give us the grace to scatter new seeds in the fields of injustice.

Lord in your mercy, hear our prayer

Ancient of Days, forgive us again when we fail to show mercy. Forgive us when we do not water the plants in our own backyards. We remember how often we have traveled to worship you in the temple for solace only and not for strength, for pardon only and not for renewal. We remember the times we did not see you in the person we called our enemy. We remember old bitterness passed on by generations who forgot the freedom of forgiveness. Unite us in the truth that love is the most powerful force for social change and teach us how to preach love in all our actions.

Lord in your mercy, hear our prayer

Loving God, you teach us that mercy is twice blessed as it
rains down on all of us. Thank you for brother sun, sister
moon, and for every creature on this earth we call Eden.
Teach us to be merciful to this fragile earth, our island home.
Teach us to overturn the hard, dry ground of our stone hearts
and remember the clay from which we were formed in the
likeness of love.

Lord in your mercy, hear our prayer

Prince of Peace, may your unbounded mercy reach even
into the fields of battle. May you strengthen the doctors
battling disease, advocates battling universal issues of
violence and institutional poverty, and protesters railing
against principalities. May you embolden those working
toward full inclusion and freedom. Give us the courage to
speak our truth, even when our voices shake. Give us the
understanding to turn our swords to ploughshares. Speak
to us through dark nights of fear and bright days of hope
of your desire for peace.

Lord in your mercy, hear our prayer

Wondrous Giver, we thank you for the inspiration and
challenge of farming. May our eyes be opened by all the gifts
of creation. Encourage us in our daily tasks to water, weed,
and do justice, show mercy, and walk humbly with you,
O God.

Lord in your mercy, hear our prayer